WILLIAM COVEL'S

A JUST AND TEMPERATE DEFENCE OF THE FIVE BOOKS OF ECCLESIASTICAL POLITY WRITTEN BY RICHARD HOOKER

WILLIAM COVEL'S

A JUST AND TEMPERATE DEFENCE OF THE FIVE BOOKS OF ECCLESIASTICAL POLITY WRITTEN BY RICHARD HOOKER

William Covel

Edited and With an Introduction
by
John A. Taylor

Texts and Studies in Religion
Volume 79

The Edwin Mellen Press
Lewiston•Queenston•Lampeter

Library of Congress Cataloging-in-Publication Data

Covell, William, d. 1614?
  [Just and temperate defence of the five books of Ecclesiastical
polity written by Richard Hooker]
  William Covel's a just and temperate defence of the five books of
Ecclesiastical polity written by Richard Hooker / William Covel ;
edited, and with an introduction, by John A. Taylor.
      p. cm. -- (Texts and studies in religion ; v. 79)
  Includes bibliographical references and index.
  ISBN 0-7734-8243-1 (hardcover)
  1. Hooker, Richard, 1553 or 4-1600. Ecclesiastical polity.
2. Church of England--Government. 3. Church polity. I. Taylor,
John A., 1942- . II. Title. III. Series.
  BV649.H83C64   1998
  262.9' 83--dc21   98-44216
                                                         CIP

This is volume 79 in the continuing series
Texts and Studies in Religion
Volume 79 ISBN 0-7734-8243-1
TSR Series ISBN 0-88946-976-8

A CIP catalog record for this book is available from the British Library.

The Edwin Mellen Press
Box 450
Lewiston, New York
USA 14092-0450

The Edwin Mellen Press
Box 67
Queenston, Ontario
CANADA L0S 1L0

The Edwin Mellen Press, Ltd.
Lampeter, Ceredigion, Wales
UNITED KINGDOM SA48 8LT

Printed in the United States of America

I dedicate this edition of Covel's work to my students
at Southern Illinois University at Edwardsville.

A Just and Temperate Defence

Of the Five Books of "Ecclesiastical Polity" Written by Richard Hooker:
Against an Uncharitable "Letter of Certain English Protestants" (As They Term
Themselves) "Craving Resolution, in Some Matters of Doctrine, Which Seem to
Overthrow the Foundation of Religion, and the Church Amongst Us."

by William Covel, D.D.

TABLE OF CONTENTS

EDITOR'S ACKNOWLEDGEMENTS

Robert Coulter patiently read the editor's preface and provided very valuable suggestions for its improvement. James Haas read the preface and rescued it from several mistakes. Sharon Hahs, dean of the College of Arts and Sciences at my home institution, Southern Illinois University at Edwardsville, generously made possible the typing of this entire manuscript. Winifred Kiszewski typed it. Edwin Lawrence twice read the preface, carefully read Covel's text, and provided detailed comment on both. Marjorie Morgan read the preface and provided splendid advice. Cathy Lynn O'Connell skillfully read the proof. I have not in every instance taken advice proffered, and the remaining errors in the editor's preface are entirely my own. Above all, I would like to thank my students, past and present, and I dedicate to them my reissue of Covel's book.

J. A. Taylor

EDITOR'S PREFACE

by John A. Taylor

This slim volume, written by William Covel, was first published in 1603.[1] Its full title is *A Just and Temperate Defence of the Five Books of "Ecclesiastical Polity" Written by Richard Hooker: Against an Uncharitable "Letter of Certain English Protestants" (As They Term Themselves) "Craving Resolution, in Some Matters of Doctrine, Which Seem to Overthrow the Foundation of Religion, and the Church Amongst Us."* Covel intended this book to be an epitome of Richard Hooker's *Of the Laws of Ecclesiastical Polity.* Covel's complete text is here reprinted. It has been set in fresh type specifically for this new edition.

In addition to introducing Covel's book, and the circumstances in which it first appeared, this preface will discuss the important role that the republication of Covel's book could now serve for British historians. First, Covel's book will illuminate their current discussion of English national identity. The field of British history has been in decline in American academic life, but now study of national identity transforms the field's perspective and, although the point is controversial, the new emphasis on national identity may lessen the difference between British and American history. Second, republication of Covel's book will provide historians with a convenient Anglican exhibit for Max Weber's theories of the Protestant ethic. Weber's theories undergo new scrutiny because their Marxist counterparts have ceased to appeal.[2] Finally, the preface contains a suggestion, a brief one, of the function of Hooker's theology in present Church of England disputes.

My suggestion will concern Hooker's borrowing from St. Thomas Aquinas and from Aristotle.[3] Covel's Article XX confessed the extensive debt to this heritage. The word *scholastic* is a seventeenth-century appellation for such borrowers. *Scholastic* appertained to Hooker, and it signified his resemblance to Aquinas and Aristotle. Sir Robert Filmer, an English follower of the French political philosopher, Jean Bodin, called Hooker one of the "profoundest scholar[s] that ever was known."[4]

Filmer named two only, "Aristotle in natural philosophy" and "Mr. Hooker in Divinity." Filmer hinted that he himself had surpassed Hooker, however. "Late writers have taken too much upon trust from the subtle Schoolmen." Adam Smith, J. S. Mill, and other nineteenth-century and twentieth-century writers echoed Filmer in suggesting that Aristotelian theory weakened Church of England theologies. Smith and Mill will appear at the conclusion of this preface.

First, here are a few words about this book and its author, William Covel. He supplied what his Greek and Latin speaking age called an enchiridion or vade-mecum, which is to say a manual or a little handbook. When Covel wrote, Richard Hooker had only just recently provided the Church of England with its lasting theological basis. Covel supplied a clear summary of the work of Richard Hooker, and, in a general way, Covel's book was also a summary of school philosophy as preserved in Protestant England not long after the Reformation. Born in Chatterton, Lancashire, Covel was a Cambridge University scholar. He graduated B.A. in 1584, proceeded M.A. in 1588, and was chosen a fellow of Queens' College, Cambridge, in July 1589. Railing against noblemen and bishops in a sermon, he irritated the episcopal authorities in 1597, but he was still awarded his D.D. degree in 1601, two years before the publication of this book, and he was collated to the prebend of All Saints, in Hungate, Lincoln, on 22 September 1612. Since his successor was nominated in 1614, one may infer that Covel's death had occurred before that date.

We know little detail about Covel himself, but we have, in his handbook, a splendid précis of Richard Hooker's long and complex tenets. The handbook is a complete and undoubtedly authentic but still mercifully brief digest. To expedite study of early seventeenth-century Anglican theologies, scholars still consult Covel's handbook in its original edition of 1603, but copies from that edition are, of course, now very scarce. Further, the 1603 edition is not easy reading. It was printed in a form that daunts the modern reader: the letter *v* often stands for the letter *u*, other spellings vary, and many more minor details differ from current usage. Of no use to scholars, and of no importance to the meaning of the text, these things are great barriers for undergraduate students. They find the 1603 edition of Covel's book to be heavy going, but that hardship is needless.

The edition here reprinted is that of Covel's nineteenth-century editor, Benjamin Hanbury.[5] Hanbury republished Covel's book with Hooker's collected works in 1830. Hanbury's notice gave Covel's treatise on Hooker a modest nineteenth-century fame. There are two reasons to reprint Hanbury's text now rather than the 1603 text. First, Hanbury modernized the type and the usages of the 1603 text. Doing so, Hanbury produced a text that serves scholars just as well as the 1603 edition, and that serves casual readers better than that 1603 edition, yet that loses nothing. Further, by irony, Hanbury's edition of Covel would perish if this present reprinting did not preserve it. Hanbury's edition is equally as scarce as the 1603 edition, and Hanbury's edition is now far more fragile than Covel's original edition. Printed on rag paper, seventeenth-century books are, on the whole, durable, while nineteenth-century books, which were printed on wood pulp paper treated with acid, are not. The pages of Hanbury's book are yellow with oxidation, and they crumble in the hand as one turns them, while the 1603 books will endure indefinitely. Covel's text is reprinted here in Hanbury's version. Covel's text is unabridged, and his footnotes are reproduced also, but not Hanbury's. They are references to other volumes of Hanbury's edition of Hooker's works.

Covel was a Church of England man. His book was, ultimately, as Hooker's had been, an effort to strengthen the Church of England by refutation of its puritan opponents. This book retains theological interest, but it is now useful to secular historians in other ways that neither Covel nor Hanbury anticipated. Two things, in particular, will attract the attention of secular historians. This preface will focus on these two points. They are national identity and the Protestant ethic.

Before that discussion, however, here are a few words about the Church of England and puritanism. This handbook still serves the purpose that Covel identified when he prepared it in the early seventeenth century, the purpose for which Hanbury valued it, the purpose of providing a brief introduction to Anglican theology and church discipline, or church government. They were the principal matters of discussion in Hooker, and Covel thought them especially important in 1603 because of the accession of King James VI of Scotland to the throne of England as King James I. The accession of King James I brought his house of Stuart to the throne. In Stuart England, theological disputes on matters such as the sacrament intermingled with secular politics. Covel feared that King James would incline to the Calvinist position. King James had imbibed Calvinist opinions in Scotland, opinions hostile to the theology and discipline of the Church of England. Covel sought to defend moderate Anglican theology and episcopal church discipline against Calvinist challenge. Covel feared the Church of England would lose its moderate Protestant theology and its discipline or government by bishops.

Perhaps some background is necessary to explain why Covel thought to defend moderate theology and episcopal church discipline at the accession of King James I. The Christian church in England was Roman Catholic until reconstructed in the time of King Edward VI, son of King Henry VIII. King Henry VIII had abolished the papal power in England, declared himself supreme head, under God, of the church, and shut down monasteries, but he did little to establish Protestant doctrine. On the contrary, King Henry VIII remained attached to Roman Catholic belief in most areas. He had bitterly persecuted the Lollard tradition native to England, a tradition that anticipated Protestant doctrine in its denial of papal supremacy, of the Roman Catholic doctrine of the sacraments, and in its translation of Christian scriptures into English. Further, King Henry had published over his name a condemnation of continental Protestantism. However, King Henry VIII allowed his son, Edward, to be raised in the Protestant view, and the boy's Protestant uncle, Lord Seymour, a zealous Protestant, became regent when King Henry died. Thomas Cranmer, Archbishop of Canterbury, established a full Protestant church in England during King Edward's reign. Cranmer wrote the *Book of Common Prayer*, two editions of which he issued during the reign, one in 1549 and one in 1552. The differences between the two editions gave faint indications of later divisions between moderate and radical English Protestants. The 1552 edition was more Calvinist. The *Book of Common Prayer*, issued again in 1559, joined with John Foxe's later *Acts and Monuments* and with the still later King James Bible, and they became the main literary props of English Protestant religious life.[6]

Zealous Protestant reformers, Seymour and Cranmer were nevertheless moderates in Protestant theology, and they were moderates also in matters of church discipline. They retained episcopacy. Cranmer had been to Germany as a young man where he had absorbed there the principal points of Martin Luther's reform program. Martin Luther was a German monk, learned in theology. Many medieval reformers challenged the corruption practiced by members of the Roman Catholic church. Luther traced the corruption to Roman Catholic theology, and, among other things, to the doctrine of soteriology, the doctrine of salvation. Roman Catholic doctrine gave great authority to priests. Luther taught the preeminence of faith over all other mediation between human and divine. He taught the priesthood of all believers. Further, seeking the protection of local princes against the jurisdiction of the Holy Roman Empire and the pope, Luther, successfully, called for secular princes to undertake reform of the church. Luther was a moderate of sorts who vehemently opposed the Anabaptists and all other reformers more radical than he. Many followed Luther in proposing reforms for the church.[7]

To understand the impact of theology on political conflicts in Covel's day, one must name the contending English parties or factions. The names here are taken from the *Oxford English Dictionary, Second Edition, on CD-Rom*. One may safely call *Anglican* those communicants who accepted royal and episcopal administration of the Elizabethan church, its clerical vestments, and its prayer book. These things gave Anglicans some unity, despite their differences on many other issues. The word *Anglican* was in use in this sense by the early seventeenth century. What to call their opponents? No single word obtained currency, though many appeared. No single word is now satisfactory. An early example of the usage of the word *puritan* is to be found in *Martin Marprelate* tracts, satirical writings that appeared in 1588 and 1589 from a secret press. The word *puritan* had an echo of medieval Cathars or Catharism. The Cathars were a group who thought themselves more pure and undefiled than ordinary Christians. Some English writers called the puritans *Brownists* after an early champion, Robert Brown, or, as Hanbury wrote the name, Browne. Brown, ironically, conformed to the Church of England. Puritans may be further divided. *Presbyterians* recognized ecclesiastically no higher order than that of a presbyter, an office they held to be identical with the *bishop* and *elder* of the new testament. Presbyters were of equal rank. Presbyterians governed each congregation by its session, and they subordinated the sessions to the presbytery, the presbyteries to the synod, and the synods to a general assembly of the church. *Congregationalists*, another term for *independent*, wished separate congregations to be self governing. Those puritans who wished to draw apart from the national Church of England were called *separatists*. These terms came into wide use in the seventeenth century. The general words *nonconformist* and *dissenter* also came to be in wide usage, but the first words are too precise for Covel's time, and *nonconformist* or *dissenter* are too broad. No single word is exact now, and *puritan* is no worse than the others, so one may use it, but with caution because it involves verbal tangles. The word, originally a term of invective, was coined, in the *Marprelate* tracts, to identify English followers of John Calvin. The word came to signify a wide range of persons who sought to reform the established Church of England or at least to rid it of the remnants of Roman Catholic practice and belief. The puritan movement had its source in exiles who fled England to Geneva in Queen Mary's reign of 1553-58. Later some of these men and women fled England for Holland and thence for Massachusetts. Others remained in England and confirmed there a division between moderate and radical Protestants, a division so bitter that it led to civil war.

The political and ecclesiastical partisans of Covel's day may be further understood, and the moderation of the Church of England made clear, if one uses the sacrament of the eucharist to catalog or sort the range of ecclesiastical persuasions after Luther's Reformation. The Roman Catholic view is that there are seven sacraments, viz., baptism, confirmation, the eucharist, penance, extreme unction, order, and matrimony, and, in the sacrament of the eucharist, a priest miraculously turns bread and wine into the body and blood of Christ. This is the famous doctrine of *transubstantiation.* By this view, only the accidents of appearance remain in the bread and wine, and their whole substance is converted. These are Aristotelian categories. Luther dropped them. He developed an equally famous doctrine of the eucharist. He said the real presence of Christ was "in and with and under" the bread and the wine. Anglicans, following Luther, usually acknowledged only two sacraments, baptism and the lord's supper. Anglicans held that these were visible signs by which God did invisible works. There was also a distinctively puritan position. Many English puritans denied that the scriptures sanctioned the Church of England position on the sacraments. These puritans abandoned the name *sacrament* entirely and used instead the word *ordinance.* They held that the ceremony of the lord's supper was a memory service, ordained by Christ, but they denied that bread and wine were means conditional and necessary to faith. Bread and wine remained unchanged during the service. This view put these puritans in conflict with the Church of England, and, especially, with Richard Hooker.

The range of Protestant opinion established itself in England, and the result was political conflict. That happened in this way. When King Edward died in 1553, his Roman Catholic sister, Queen Mary I, ascended to the throne. She abolished King Edward's Protestant reforms and returned England to the papal jurisdiction. Many English Protestants fled abroad, while more than 300 others were martyred at home under Queen Mary's rule.[8] Of these Marian exiles, some went to Frankfurt in Germany, and others went to Geneva where John Calvin led his reform. John Calvin was a French theologian, born at Noyon in 1509, and trained at Paris in the law. While the differences between Luther and Calvin were often not seen to be great on the continent of Europe, the subsequent Anglican and puritan positions, which retained echoes of Lutheranism and Calvinism, became very far apart in England. Queen Mary's effort to return England to papal allegiance came at an unfortunate time. Quarrels in the Roman Catholic world prevented her great servant, Cardinal Pole, from achieving very much in England.

English Protestants had quarreled little with one another in a partisan way before Queen Mary's reign, but Protestant conflict embroiled Marian exiles in Europe and was clearly present in England thereafter. Queen Mary died in 1558, and her sister, Elizabeth, came to the throne as Queen Elizabeth. She established Protestant reforms permanently in England. The Marian exiles returned. They brought the European range of English Protestant opinion with them, and it replaced Roman Catholicism as the source of conflicted counsel. Debates between Protestants became a main factor in English politics, for the controversy on theology and on the sacraments served in England to divide former exiles into parties with different views on other issues, especially on church government or discipline. How to replace the pope's government of the church with that of the prince? If one denied the real presence of Christ in the sacrament, then one also denied that the Christian church had priests set apart from ordinary believers. From that denial, came the complaint against distinctive clerical vestments. A step further, and the denial led to a disciplinary notion that the individual congregations should allow conscience to guide them on matters of church governance.

Queen Elizabeth's favoring of ecclesiastical moderates divided her Protestant subjects and made their ecclesiastical differences into political differences. Queen Elizabeth personally sympathized with Lutherans in religion[9] because she prized in particular their tendency, similar to Luther's, to submit the Christian church to governance by the godly secular prince. She patronized therefore moderate theologies and monarchical and episcopal church organization after her accession. English Calvinists thought she had insufficiently reformed the Church of England, and, as Robert Brown said, Calvinists lacked the patience to tarry while her secular government resolved the matter.

The range of Protestant opinion had been partisan from the beginning of the reign of Queen Elizabeth. The *Marprelate* tracts published the conflict. They had a violent and vituperative tone, and government reaction was harsh. Most Elizabethan Protestants thought moderate ecclesiastical reform by the government sufficient, and even most puritans accepted a royal role in church discipline, but puritans also objected to the following: the use of clerical vestments similar to those worn by Roman Catholic prelates; the use of the cross in baptism; confirmation; the ring in marriage; the profanation of the lord's day; bowing at the name of Jesus; the reading of the apocrypha in lessons; and to the compulsory use of Cranmer's *Book of Common Prayer*.[10]

We may understand the conflict of Protestant opinion better if we resolve part of the verbal tangle that, as was said earlier, besets study of English puritanism. We may do so by concentration on Thomas Cartwright, who, no doubt, wrote the letter that Covel refuted. Cartwright was the single most important opponent of the Elizabethan settlement. He lived from 1535-1603. That he was the principal opponent of the Elizabethan settlement is proved by Archbishop John Whitgift's honoring Cartwright with long and detailed refutation of Cartwright's views.[11] Hooker also wrote to oppose the doctrines of Cartwright who was Lady Margaret Professor Divinity at the University of Cambridge.

Cartwright was a founder of congregationalism. Queen Mary's accession forced Cartwright to leave the University of Cambridge, and he spent the interval in work connected with the common law. His experience with the law may have tempered and moderated his hostility toward the Elizabethan settlement of religion, and his moderation made him a formidable opponent. He shirked the word puritan himself, but he thought that the chief points of Roman Catholic doctrine were disguised in the Church of England by its show of inveighing against puritans. Puritan or no himself, Cartwright surely defied government more effectively than most Elizabethan puritans. Cartwright was also a powerful preacher, and his friends told with pride a story about his preaching at Great St. Mary's, one of the largest churches in Cambridge, and surely the most illustrious, outside the university. They said that the warden feared for the stained glass windows because the crowd, gathered to hear Cartwright preach, packed the church. It was so full that people began to climb the walls. Cartwright was deprived of his professorship at Cambridge in 1570. He made his was to Geneva where he perfected his knowledge of John Calvin's work. In England, the crucial impact of Calvinism was that its doctrine of private conscience encouraged people to resist episcopal church discipline.

We have used the doctrines on the eucharist to explain the range of Protestant opinion in Covel's day. While the question of the eucharist was vital, however, to understand Cartwright's impact upon English episcopacy, we must also examine another matter, the question of the power and scope, the sufficiency, of human reason. As Cartwright reminded the authorities, the question of the scope of human reason bore on church discipline. Protestant opinions concerning the scope or power of human reason also formed a panorama.

Cartwright said that the Church of England inferred that reason gained from nature some knowledge that was necessary to salvation. He suggested that scripture contained all knowledge necessary to salvation.[12] If one said, with Cartwright, that human reason was no guide to God's justice, then knowledge of absolute morality was not rational. Private conscience, informed by grace, became the only human faculty able to direct human action aright. This was Calvin's doctrine.[13] The human understanding is "sluggish," said Calvin, and natural events seem fortuitous, though in fact their causes lie hidden in God's purpose. Calvin also rejected any notion of fate or chance in the direction of human affairs.[14] He attributed all actions to the providence of God, and he quoted St. Augustine on that matter. Even though events, on this view, are caused only by the will of God, yet that cause is often hidden from human eyes. Calvin denied that human wisdom may discern or prompt the purposes of providence. He held that St. Augustine was wrong to think providence compatible with human free will. Humans, however, seem to themselves to deal with fortune, and humans therefore seem to exercise free will in so doing, for, since events "bear on the face of them no other appearance," they seem fortuitous "according to our knowledge and judgment." Free will, however, is an attribute of God alone. Only

God can save or damn souls. Free will does not ground human moral responsibility. Human beings are guilty of sin even though they have no free will to ground their guilt. "The perfect qualities of a moral agent are in God," as the American Jonathan Edwards said later.

Cartwright's firm Calvinist opinions were in sharp contrast to the emollient doctrine on the Anglican side. Covel said, for the Anglicans, that the church of God was a company of faith where the word of God was duly preached and the sacraments rightly administered. This was a crucial and emollient statement. Most puritans could accept that definition more easily than they could the other Anglican view that *church* meant *people* and that, therefore, all English people were subject to the English church just as they were to the common law. Covel's phrase was a standard one that offered puritans an olive branch. It allowed Anglicans to share with puritans a definition of the Christian church, and, if continued, Anglican moderation might have alleviated some puritan choler in the reign of King Charles I.[15]

Yet *might have* are sad words. The emollient definition of the church occurred, in Covel, within a context that belied puritan emphasis on conscience. Covel allowed no claim of private conscience against the standard of reason, and he allowed the prayer book, grounded in reason and scripture (and not individual conscience), to establish right preaching and right administration of the sacraments. Covel was very clear what he was about. He denounced those who would disown all human reasoning by imputing "a stoical and fatal Necessity." He claimed that Calvin had misunderstood human reason and human free will. Hooker had held that human reason was able to grasp the law of nature, though not the mind of God, and Anglicans used a limited freedom of the will as a ground of human moral responsibility. Covel was even clearer than Hooker on these points, especially on the scope of human reason. Acknowledging Calvin as one of the most eminent men the French church had ever produced, and agreeing partially with Calvin, Covel thought human reason much diminished by the fall into sin, but human reason retained still some powers of interpretation. Those powers were essential. "As the Schoolmen say," Covel remarked, "man standeth in need of a threefold Law," eternal, natural, and human, and knowledge of natural law establishes a role for human reason. Christian scripture was not needed to establish natural laws. For Christians, said Covel, scripture was, however, a great aid to establishing the role proper to human reason.

Covel used the doctrine of the trinity to illustrate his points about reason. So crushing to puritanism did he believe the argument about the trinity to be that he put it almost at the beginning of his book. Human reason could not arrive at the doctrine of the trinity from nature, Covel said. Scripture was necessary. On the other hand, while scripture mentioned the three persons of the trinity, it nowhere contained an explicit statement of the doctrine. Informed or aided by scripture, human reason could grasp the doctrine. Covel taunted puritans that their views of human reason would not yield solid support for the trinity, and he viewed this as proof of Hooker's theological superiority. Covel must have remembered that Calvin's Geneva would burn a theologian who called into question the doctrine of the trinity.

So important were these theological quarrels to secular politics, that the text of *The Laws of Ecclesiastical Polity* became a matter of political dispute. Covel's book contributes to discussion of this important point. Hooker edited the first five books himself, but the last three of the eight were issued only in 1662 after the restoration of King Charles II. Isaac Walton wrote a life of Hooker for that edition, and many later editions of Hooker reprinted Walton's biography. Hanbury reprinted Walton, for instance. The textual problems with these last three books have exercised many scholars. Deliberately distorted information was supplied to Isaac Walton. Was Hooker's text also altered to support the views of people in 1662? In particular, two issues stood out, monarchy and the eucharist. The eighth book exalted monarchy. Hooker said it was rooted in biblical injunctions. He counseled submission to royal government of the church and the state as the children of Israel had been submitted by God to government by their Kings in both secular and sacred matters. Hooker also took a view of the eucharist closer to Lutheran, and even

Roman Catholic, opinion than was comfortable for puritans. Was Hooker's text altered in 1662 to strengthen these views? Historian Peter Laslett found evidence that Hooker's text was already by the late 1630s much as it appeared when printed in 1662.[16] Laslett inferred that the 1662 text could not have been far from Hooker's intent. Covel says at the very end of his book that he had from Hooker himself word that Hooker had completed the final three books of his great work. Covel's testimony strengthens Laslett's case. Long regarded as an Olympian writer whose work was high above the controversy of his day, Hooker was instead a partisan writer who deliberately supported government.

While Hanbury was not aware of the problems with Walton's biography of Hooker, Hanbury, however, was very well aware that a great value of Covel's book was its near proximity in time to Hooker's writing. Covel's commentary on Hooker was free of later seventeen-century concerns. As Hanbury pointed out, Covel's book arose from his interest in a specific puritan critique of Hooker's doctrine, *A Christian Letter*. Thomas Cartwright was the reputed author of this letter. Hanbury says that Hooker intended to answer this letter himself, but death prevented his doing so, a death "hastened" by puritan defamation in the letter. The letter said that Hooker thought of himself as chief rabbi. The letter even hinted that Hooker had mistaken himself for Christ. Covel attacked the letter at length in the beginning of his book. Hanbury discussed and, in fragments, reprinted this letter in his edition of Hooker's *works*. The letter is not reprinted here as it is already available in a modern edition. The principal points of the letter concerned the following: the trinity; the sufficiency of scripture to the realization and preserving of spiritual health; the superior warrant of scripture when contradicted by the traditions of the church; a disavowal of human free will; affirmation of the supreme importance of faith; all excellence the work of God alone; God's righteousness independent of human works and especially works of supererogation; sin; predestination; the visible and the invisible church; preaching; ordination of clergy; and sacraments.

Covel did not foresee the later challenges to Hooker's text, and Covel had only the clear and present danger of puritanism in mind. Covel had little use for the Roman Catholic viewpoint, but he did not bother refuting it. Puritanism was his business, and refutation of Cartwright's letter. Covel explicitly said in his own title that he commented on the first five books of Hooker's masterpiece, and Covel did not have the passages on monarchy and eucharist that later Protestants found difficult. For Hanbury, too, Covel's value lay only in his ability to clarify Hooker's position in the controversies with Elizabeth puritans. Opposition to Cartwright's theology and church discipline gave Anglicans Hooker's theology. Opposition to Cartwright also impelled Covel to write. Hanbury gave particular attention to Cartwright.

Covel feared the Christian letter because it might incline King James to the Calvinist position. King James had imbibed Calvinist opinions in Scotland, opinions hostile to the theology and discipline of the Church of England. Covel feared that King James would undo the work of Queen Elizabeth. Covel feared that the Church of England would lose its moderate Protestant theology and its discipline or government by bishops. Covel's fears were needless. No one understood better than King James the secular political issues that hinged in England on theological disputes. To abolish church government by bishops, in the king's view, would threaten monarchy itself. Covel was wrong to fear that King James would favor puritans. The king was more Anglican than the Anglicans.

For Hanbury, and for his nineteenth-century co-religionists, heirs of puritanism, these Elizabethan debates over episcopacy remained living issues. Hanbury was a distinguished student of the independent or congregational religious tradition.[17] These doctrinal controversies still have force for some people now, and they still find Covel's text helpful. Anyone interested in understanding the history and evolution of Anglicanism will find Covel helpful. I will return to this point at the end of this essay.

Summarizing and praising Hooker's new theology, Covel meant to underscore the doctrinal strengths of the Church of England. He meant to establish the partisan position of the Church of England among the ranges of party opinion that

Protestantism brought to England. The Church of England before Hooker's day, and Covel's, too often had clear policy but no clear theological doctrine. Political exigency had created and defined the Church of England. Puritans were critical of the Church of England for this cause. They ascribed to a political exigency Queen Elizabeth's limited and partial reformation of the Church of England. By appeal to Hooker and, through him, to scholastic philosophical doctrine, Covel sought to make the Elizabethan settlement seem sound, proper, scriptural, and doctrinal. He anticipated bitter political quarrels over English royal and episcopal church discipline in the reign of King James.

How do the issues of the sacrament and of free will touch Max Weber's interpretation of later British modernization? How do these issues touch historians' current discussion of British national identity? Hooker's is the better statement of Anglican doctrine, no doubt, but that text is long, and the complexities of its interpretation present a needless cul-de-sac. Covel supplied a summary of Hooker's text. Covel's brief and clear summary is better suited to the needs of current analysis. The importance of Covel's text for Weber's thesis will be a major remaining point in this preface. We turn first, however, to the use of Covel's text in the current discussion of British national identity.

David Cannadine, Linda Colley, Gerald Newman, and Benedict Anderson began much of the present debate about British national identity.[18] Their views have transformed the field or academic discipline of British history. While their work has concentrated especially on the eighteenth century and the nineteenth century, the sixteenth century and the seventeenth century have to be seen anew in light of their work.

Anderson's *Imagined Communities* described the American Revolution as the key episode in the construction of national identity. The title phrase was Anderson's substitute for "nationalism," which is "notoriously difficulty to define." He said that national identities were constructed or imagined by authors and other intellectuals. This happened first in the American Revolution and subsequently in France, South

America, and elsewhere in Europe. The American Revolution constructed American national identity. French soldiers and others brought those ideas to France where the French Revolution established them. In the case of Britain, the American Revolution sparked the construction of British identity. Anderson intended to refute Marxists, and he did so with great wit. He said that the rise of nationalism was the nemesis of Marxism. He also refuted the great failure of those, whom he called liberals, who believed that political liberty characterized American and British societies and accounted for their economic successes. Anderson said Marxism and liberalism failed together.

Anderson placed great stress on language. He said that in the case of Europe the Latin language remained a strong antidote to parochial thought. The use of vernaculars, and the appearance of cheap paper and the steam press, greatly accelerated the spread of reading matter. Religious and dynastic identities were still dominant before the American and French Revolutions, and nationalism has been dominant since that time.

A general viewpoint concerning the central importance of national identity was quickly established in the field of British history, at least in the United States, but historians now differ acrimoniously about its details. Many American students of British history find in national identity a dominant and controlling explanation, but, even so, these historians differ on details, especially details about chronology. Newman had priority in the description of many details of the argument, and he continued to assert with forceful words the correctness of his views. He held that eighteenth-century British aristocrats were sophisticated cosmopolitans who, like Lawrence Sterne, thought the French ordered many things better than the English. Newman held that many ordinary and fewer sophisticated English people were deeply xenophobic in the eighteenth century. They hated the French as national and as religious enemies. Roman Catholicism was a trigger for English hatred of France. Ordinary English people hated the French before the French Revolution, and that event redoubled their loathing. The French Revolution forced British aristocrats to join in the popular condemnation of France and the French, and this new British consensus underlay a new national identity.

Linda Colley's revision of Benedict Anderson's work on nationalism provided a another framework for British history. For Colley, British national identity was constructed long before the American Revolution, just after 1688, in fact, and more precisely after 1707. The English persuaded other British Protestants to coalesce on the basis of their sharing the essential points of Protestant religion. The glorious revolution of 1688 allowed moderate Protestant theologies to become the basis for an English absorption of the other regional communities into a larger Protestant and British identity. The English appealed to them to form a common British front on the basis of moderate Protestantism. This worked well for the short term, since Britain united against its continental Roman Catholic enemies, especially France, but the system was a long term prescription for region tension. Protestantism as nationalism condemned Ireland to an oppressive occupation.

J.C.D. Clark, in a brilliant historiographical review, argued against these uses of British national identity. He said that national identity explanations are American treatments of British history, ones calculated to save the field of British history in America by making it more amenable to American taste.[19] Clark thought the notion had far less appeal in Britain than in America.

Covel's work illuminates this discussion of national identity. Covel provides all sides with an important example of what one means by Anglicanism. Those historians who hold, with Newman and Colley, that British national identity was constructed on the basis of moderate Protestantism will therefore look for a handy summary of Anglican theologies. They may find it in Covel's book. No other brief statement of theology is so well suited as Covel's for present-day historical analysis of the moderate Protestant basis of British national identity. In laying down clearly an authentic Anglican theology, Covel, for these present-day historians, also constructed identity. No subsequent statement of Anglican views attained the prestige and authority of Richard Hooker's, and Covel's nearly contemporary summary is valuable for its brevity and accuracy.

Covel's national purpose was even clearer than Hooker's. Covel wrote on the occasion of a royal accession. Covel wrote to counter a puritan writing, and he wrote to please a king. Covel's *Defence* was proof that Anglicanism did not evolve into a national doctrine. Anglicanism began in the early sixteenth century, and continued through the seventeenth century, as a confession whose theology had been adapted to a national agenda. The national agenda dictated compromise, and compromise meant efforts to find a middle way, to offer a latitude for tender conscience, and to assert a priority of the liturgy over dogma. Covel reconstructed Anglicanism deliberately, openly, in order to facilitate British Protestant unity. King James was Scottish. Covel wrote to persuade a Protestant Scottish king whom he thought might be hostile to a purely English church. King James confirmed the basic line of thought given by Hooker and Covel, and the king's thinking was as British as that of any later English sovereign. These points should recommend Covel to current scholars. Whether one sees Anglicanism as the basis of a constructed national identity or not, one must grant that Anglicanism itself was constructed for national purposes.

Covel's book, however, also lends support to Clark's views: one must modify the argument about national identity. Since Covel's Anglicanism was British, it makes doubtful Colley's claim that 1707 was a watershed date. Why not 1603? Or earlier? The Protestant Reformation had from its origins a distinctive national flavor. "I was born for my Germans, and them will I serve," said Luther. The followers of Richard Cox in Frankfurt insisted they "would have the face of an English Church."[20] Hooker and Covel merely carried on the same Reformation tradition. They desired to make an English national Protestantism.

Covel's book is also of use in a second major historical controversy. Historians who use Max Weber's theory of the Protestant ethic, pro or con, will also find Covel's book a gem. It supplies evidence for discussion of Weber's thesis, and its supply of that evidence constitutes an important purpose for reprinting Covel's text. Weber was a German social theorist of the early twentieth century. His ideas are of particular use in interpretation of modernization. Weber said that the Protestant Reformation was a precursor of modernity, and that the Reformation produced two versions of Protestantism, one more suited to modernization than the other. This was so because Calvinist or puritan Protestantism was conducive to development of a modern personality, a frame of mind that involved a work ethic. Calvinists held the view that salvation depended neither on human works nor on the sacraments of the church. God was the sole source of salvation, and God's ways were unknowable to men and women. None of them was sure of salvation. In consequence, their predicament was one of great anxiety. This produced in them what Weber called worldly asceticism, a propensity to labor. Weber argued that unprecedented inner loneliness resulted from Calvinist religion. Sanction for greed was not the issue. Greed existed in all past civilizations, as did a propensity to labor motivated by greed. Calvinists labored without monetary reward as the principal motive. Because Calvinist men and women were unable to resolve anxiety about their moral condition, they found that anxiety impelled them to labor.[21] When they found success there, they also found solace, for they hoped, although without joy in material goods as such, that success was a sign of favor.

I should announce my own view on the matters of national identity and Weberian analysis.[22] I write as a historian and offer only my historical judgement and my proposals for the future. Of course, I leave them open for the judgements of others.

I think the English established a national identity in the Protestant Reformation, and they did so on the basis of a moderate Protestantism. Further, English Protestantism was constructed from the first to suit the needs of a polity with complex regional and sectarian diversity. The year 1707 was, however, an important date. The terrible religious strife of the seventeenth century confirmed in many Protestant minds the need to accommodate national diversity, and the heyday of Latitudinarian Protestantism coincided with, and provided the basis for, the creation of a united kingdom of all Britain. The English persuaded other British Protestants to form a united front against Roman Catholic Europe, but the English offered a broader toleration to dissenting opinion than ever one could have expected in the sixteenth century or the seventeenth century. I have one important change to suggest. I have argued elsewhere that Anglicanism itself was not the basis of a constructed British national identity. Instead, Anglicanism supported a notion of civil liberty, and this notion of civil liberty became the basis of national identity.

I am also Weberian in a general way. Weber said Anglicans were less likely than Calvinists to develop worldly asceticism. We have seen this confirmed in Covel's Anglican attitude toward human reason and toward the sacraments. Thinking more highly of human reason than did Calvinists, Anglicans did not make themselves prone to the anxiety that begot worldly asceticism. Covel illustrates this point perfectly. He said clearly that reason could guide the human will and that was the basis of moral responsibility. Anglicans also could find comfort in the power of the sacrament to communicate grace. Covel explicitly made these points. His little book is so brief and so clear that it stands out, among Anglican writings, as preeminently suited for analysis on the Weberian and national identity models.

I think Weber's theory clarifies the considerable scholarly literature which now discusses the decline of Britain.[23] Margaret Thatcher, the Tory prime minister, gave political currency to these scholarly notions, and Tony Blair, the current Labour prime minister, evidently shares her view. Britain is said to have experienced a rapid decline in recent years, and there is lively debate as to the causes and the beginning dates. Writers differ, and W.D. Rubinstein disagrees with almost the whole decline argument, but many historians think, with Correlli Barnett, that the terrible trauma of the 1939-45 war preserved in Britain the values of a traditional society. Schools scanted modern science, and industry and labor unions avoided the introduction of modern production techniques.

One should combine Weberian analysis with national identity analysis and apply the combination to the question of British decline. One can combine national identity theory with Weberian theory as follows. If Britain constructed an Anglican national identity, as many historians now say, and if, as Weber said, Calvinism was more suited to modernization than was Anglicanism, then it follows clearly that Anglicanism is the source of British ambivalence about the completion of modernization. However, worldly asceticism is not the only issue. Calvinism was a precursor of modernization because Calvinist insistence on the role of private conscience was a precursor of a better theory of civil liberty. Further, as I have said, national identity theory must be amended to make Protestant notions of civil liberty (not Protestantism itself) the basis of British national identity.

I promised at the beginning to discuss, briefly, the present proper role of Richard Hooker's theology in the Church of England. There can be no doubt that Hooker was the source of much past pride in English theological circles. Not for nothing did Filmer praise Hooker and bracket him with Aristotle. There can be no doubt, either, that Covel's presentation was an apt and accurate summary of Hooker. I submit that Covel's view is obsolete, and so is Hooker's. The theology is outmoded because it is contrary to capitalism. Puritan sanction for private conscience foreshadowed a notion of moral restraint that is now essential for capitalist economic theory. The Church of England should sanction that notion of moral restraint. In this regard, Hooker and Covel were prescient to insist that the church be ruled by the needs of society.

Britain is undergoing a massive shift toward a sanction for self-interest. The shift began in 1979, with the advent of Margaret Thatcher to Downing Street, and the shift continues now under the present Labour ministry. The shift is away from traditional notions of reason as a guide to absolute morality. The shift is toward a greater sanction for private conscience even when claims of conscience merely screen self-interested actions. In these last days, the Church of England will cling at its peril to Covel's outmoded theology. The Church of England may be disestablished.[24]

The obsolescence of Covel's theory of moral restraint appears clearly from a comparison of it with notions of moral restraint and civil liberty in Adam Smith's *Theory of Moral Sentiments.*[25] "Adam Smith set out to replace the Aristotelian philosophy of Western Europe, which had become a hinderance to liberty and economic growth."[26]   J.S. Mill's *Utilitarianism* provided a second basis for unfavorable comparison with Covel. Recall Covel on moral restraint. He echoed Aristotle and the scholastics. Covel said that reason and free will were the moral restraints needed for civil society. He argued that civil liberty required that individuals voluntarily sacrifice their private interests and desires for the sake of an absolute morality authenticated by reason but found in nature and scripture. Calvinists had said that reason was not able to discover absolute morality. They argued for the sanctity of idiosyncratic private conscience. Smith's notion of moral restraint was similar to the Calvinist one. Smith said that moral restraints were involuntary and irrational. Mill brought the argument to its conclusion. He said that moral restraints resided either in circumstances external to the mind or in subjective emotion. "The ultimate sanction, therefore, of all morality (external motives apart)," Mill said, is "a subjective feeling in our own minds."[27]

The Church of England may reconstruct its theories of moral restraint. It may abandon the notion that reason finds an absolute morality in nature and scripture. The church may make moral restraints and constraints to be two things. First is external motive (fear of the force of the state or desire for its reward), and second is individual conscience, even though conscience is subjective and idiosyncratic, and even though claims of conscience usually cloak mere personal desires and selfish interests. The church need not require individuals to recognize any moral restraint other than external motive or private conscience.

Here is a detailed exposition. Covel used the conventional language of the universities to discuss the question of civil liberty. The question is, what civil or moral restraints and constraints are needed for society? By this language, liberty is merely the absence of restraint or constraint. Restraint means that one is hindered or prevented from doing something, and constraint means that one is compelled to do something. Liberty is the absence of this hindrance or this compulsion. Natural liberty is the absence of all restraints and constraints save those of nature. A woman or man may wish to live forever, but nature restrains her or him. So natural liberty has restraints and constraints. Civil liberty has in addition the restraints and constraints needed for civil society. These restraints and constraints are called civil or moral ones. Anglicanism supplied the notions of moral or civil restraint as follows. Reason, while impaired by sin, is sufficient to direct moral choice, although reason, acting upon nature, yields only knowledge of natural law. Further, scripture supplements the light that nature gives to human reason, so the ground of moral responsibility is all that more safe and secure. Covel denounced the notion that necessity entirely bound the human will. He also sketched a scope for human liberty. All unforced actions are voluntary, he said. Supplemented by scripture, reason, therefore, is a basis for voluntary action. Reason and free will are moral restraints.

Smith and Mill solved the problem of civil liberty very much more persuasively. Avoiding the need for human reason to know absolute morality, Smith said that moral restraint must depend on force, and the circumstances of the society may direct the use of force. An invisible hand will provide a restraint, even though individuals exercise neither voluntary or rational restraint. That argument is the core of capitalism. Society may leave greed and rapacity unchecked, for greed and rapacity will generate their own restraints spontaneously. Although moral restraints were merely subjective impulses, said Mill, men and women could nevertheless sympathize with one another on the basis of such subjective impulses. Men and women could then calculate the sums of subjective human happiness. They could arrange objectively civil society's use of force so that society permitted the maximum sum of subjective human happiness. Society may acknowledge that individual judgments of social circumstances will be involuntary and irrational. Force aside, such involuntary and irrational judgments of social circumstances were the only moral restraints.

The Church of England may abandon Hooker's notion of moral restraint, and Covel's. There would be no shame in doing so. Hooker undertook work to please Queen Elizabeth, and Covel wrote to persuade King James. Doing so, Hooker and

Covel unwittingly anticipated Smith and Mill in the belief that theories of moral restraint must reflect the circumstances of society. Hooker and Covel were wrong only in their efforts to adapt a supposedly absolute notion of morality to the needs of society. Following the examples of Hooker and Covel, the church may without shame now hear the nation's new sovereign, public opinion.

Public opinion now requires a theory of moral restraint and civil liberty suited to capitalism. The proper theory of moral restraint acknowledges morality to be subjective for the individual, and the theory makes social utility a proper yardstick for civil liberty. The church may sanction this theory of moral restraint. The church may sanction self-interest, may allow private conscience as moral restraint, and may allow society to make the sum of subjective human happiness a test of social policy. The Church of England may do so. In fact, law may require it to do so.[28] I think it should do so cheerfully.

It should do so cheerfully because Anglican arguments about moral restraint and civil liberty have always been adapted to the needs of civil society. Hooker and Covel adapted their arguments to that purpose long ago. By asserting a moderate Protestant affirmation of human reason and natural law, they served current political purposes. They did so sincerely. They were right to do so. The moderation and stability of British national life has been due in large measure to the ground of British national identity in notions of civil liberty. Notions of civil liberty have changed. Failure to keep pace with changing notions of civil liberty will dissolve the connection between the Church of England and national identity. That dissolution is unthinkable.

NOTES

1.   William Covel, *A Just and Temperate Defence of the Five Books of "Ecclesiastical Polity" Written by Richard Hooker: Against an Uncharitable "Letter of Certain English Protestants" (As They Term Themselves) "Craving Resolution, in Some Matters of Doctrine, Which Seem to Overthrow the Foundation of Religion, and the Church Amongst Us* (London: Knight, 1603). See also William Covel, "A Modest and Reasonable Examination of Some Things in Use in the Church of England, 1604," excerpted in Lawrence A. Sasek, ed., *Images of English Puritanism* (Baton Rouge: Louisiana State University Press, 1989), pp. 224-237; Sasek provided a brief introduction.

2.   Markku Peltonen, *Classical Humanism and Republicanism in English Political Thought 1570-1640* (Cambridge: Cambridge University Press, 1995), for instance, engagedWeberian notions anew. Peltonen suggested that classical humanism played a more important role than Calvinism in the construction of English political discourse.

3.   Peter Munz, *The Place of Hooker in the History of Thought* (Westport, Conn.: Greenwood Press, 1971), esp. p. 56. Born in Exeter about 1554 and educated at Corpus Christi College, Oxford, Hooker lived until 1600. He is still the foremost Church of England theologian. I think Hooker's mistake, and Covel's also, was to retain so much scholastic theory. Munz detailed at length Hooker's profound theological dependence on St. Thomas and on Aristotle. "[Hooker] might have said with St. Thomas: '*Gratia non tollit naturam sed perficit.*' He could now put his finger on exactly that point where the Puritan argument according to him failed: it did not achieve a distinction between nature and supernature and the respective human faculties." Munz wrote before the current debate about Hooker's political character, but Munz suggested many things very important to that argument: Hooker wrote for an England in which radical Protestantism, or Calvinism, claimed much for private conscience and disparaged both human reason and natural law; we distort Hooker's achievement if we believe he consciously intended subsequent Anglicanism; instead, Hooker scavenged scholastic philosophy for a moderate Protestant theory of natural law and human reason, one that he opposed to Calvin's view of private conscience. Recent scholarship made clear the distinctive political nature of Hooker's discourse and its long term importance. "Hooker's writings suggest a distinctive political discourse, which Hobbes and Locke conceptualize more particularly." Thus, Stephen L. Collins *From Divine Cosmos to Sovereign State: An Intellectual History of Consciousness and the Idea of Order in Renaissance England* (New York: Oxford University Press, 1989), p. 92; see also Richard Hooker, *Of the Laws*

of Ecclesiastical Polity, ed. A. S. McGrade (Cambridge: Cambridge University Press, 1994), pp. xiii-xxx. Seventeenth-century English Calvinists often called Hooker's political theory *Erastian*. They meant to denigrate it and were wrong to do so. Hooker was sincere in his theology and deeply learned in his philosophy, but he also consciously served political ends. Calvinist theories of private conscience now appear more durable than Hooker's obsolete scholastic theories of natural law and human reason, but, in contrast, Hooker's allowing theology to serve political ends, and his recognition of the changing needs of society, I shall argue at the end of this preface, have much to offer us. He was truly prescient.

4. Sir Robert Filmer, *Patriarcha*, ed. Peter Laslett (Oxford: Blackwell, 1949), p. 55. See also Sir Robert Filmer, *Patriarcha and Other Writings*, ed. Johann P. Sommerville (Cambridge: Cambridge University Press, 1991); and Julian H. Franklin, *Jean Bodin and the Sixteenth-Century Revolution in the Methodology of Law and History* (New York: Columbia University Press, 1966).

5. Richard Hooker, *Works*, ed. Benjamin Hanbury, 3 vols. (London: Holdsworth and Ball, 1830), II:449-568. Hanbury lived from 1778 to 1864. Hanbury thought Covel's book admirably suited for inclusion in Hooker's *Works* as Covel summarized Hooker. Covel's summary was both succinct and nearly contemporary with Hooker's text.

6. *The Book of Common Prayer 1559*, ed. John E. Booty (Washington: Folger, 1982).

7. See Martin Luther, *Selected Political Writings*, ed. J. M. Porter (Philadelphia: Fortress, 1974); and Ulrich Zwingli, *Selected Works*, ed. S. M. Jackson (Philadelphia: University of Pennsylvania Press, 1972).

8. "A convincing account of the religious history of Mary's reign has yet to be written. More than any other period of Tudor history, the five years from her accession to her death have been discussed in value-laden terms which reveal the persistence of a Protestant historiography." Thus, Eamon Duffy, *The Stripping of the Altars: Traditional Religion in England c.1400- c.1580* (New Haven: Yale University Press, 1992), p. 524. Two points have been especially controversial, the fate of English Protestants at home under Queen Mary and the conditions abroad for those whom she forced into exile. As for those at home, Roland H. Bainton, *The Reformation of the Sixteenth Century* (Boston: Beacon, 1952), p. 204, quoted a contemporary witness to say that 288 were burned and others "died of famine in sundry prisons," but Protestant opinion made the totals much higher, and Queen Mary's own servants

boasted that they had forced a total of 30,000 Protestants to submit, be burned, or flee; see A. G. Dickens, *The English Reformation* (New York: Schocken, 1965), p. 265. The conditions of exile have also perplexed historians, in particular, events in Frankfurt. The small English congregation there quarreled bitterly. Calvinists, led by the famous John Knox, then straight from Geneva, and moderate Protestants, led by Richard Cox, almost came to physical conflict. See A. G. Dickens and Dorothy Carr, eds., *The Reformation in England to the Accession of Elizabeth I* (London: Edward Arnold, 1971), pp. 155-157; and Jasper Ridley, *John Knox* (Oxford: Oxford University Press, 1968), pp. 189-214. Ridley counted 800 English Protestant exiles by the spring of 1554.

9. Hirofumi Horie, "The Lutheran Influence on the Elizabethan Settlement, 1558-1563," *The Historical Journal*, 34, 3 (1991), pp. 519-537; see esp. pp. 522-523. "Elizabeth herself inclined towards this Lutheran Confession, which could probably be identified in England with the 1549 Prayer Book. . . . On the domestic side she knew quite well that some sort of compromise with the reformers had to be worked out, and here she wanted to find a point of compromise closer to the Prayer book of 1549 than that of 1552."

10. The list is from a petition, presented to King James I in 1603, called the Millenary Petition because a thousand English clergy were said to have signed it. J.R. Tanner, *Constitutional Documents of the Reign of James I 1603-1625* (Cambridge: Cambridge University Press, 1961), pp. 50 and 56. The petition expressed the views of Thomas Cartwright. The king summoned a conference at Hampton Court to discuss the points raised by the petition, but death prevented Cartwright from attending.

11. John Whitgift, *Works*, ed. John Ayre (Cambridge: Cambridge University Press, 1851). See also Patrick Collinson, *The Elizabethan Puritan Movement* (Berkeley and Los Angeles: University of California Press, 1967).

12. Thomas Cartwright (reputed author), *A Christian Letter of Certain English Protestants, Unfained fauours of the present State of Religion, Authorized and Professed in England: unto that Reverend and Learned Man, Mr. R. Hoo. Requiring Resolution in Certain Matters of Doctrine* (New York: Da Capo Press, 1969), pp. 7-8.

13. Cartwright, *Christian Letter*, p. 37.

14. John Calvin, *Institutes of the Christian Religion*, ed. John T. McNeill, trans. Ford Lewis Battles, 2 vols. (Philadelphia: Westminster, 1960), esp. I:197-228. See also David Steinmetz, *Calvin in Context* (Oxford: Oxford

xxx

University Press, 1995), pp. 47-8.

15. Conrad Russell, *The Fall of the British Monarchies 1637-1642* (Oxford: Oxford University Press, 1991), pp. 19-20, pointed out that the thirty-nine articles repeated exactly Calvin's doctrine of the church: "The visible church of Christ is a congregation of faithful men, in the which the pure word of God is preached, and the sacraments be duly ministered according to Christ's ordinance in all those things that of necessity are requisite to the same."

16. Filmer, *Patriarcha*, p. 83.

17. See Benjamin Hanbury, *Historical Memorials Relating to the Independents or Congregationalists*, 3 vols. (London: The Congregational Union of England and Wales, 1839-1844).

18. Benedict Anderson, *Imagined Communities: Reflections on the Origin and Spread of Nationalism* (London: Verso, 1991); David Cannadine, *Aspects of Aristocracy* (New Haven: Yale University Press, 1994); Linda Colley, *Britons: Forging the Nation, 1707-1837* (New Haven: Yale University Press, 1992); Gerald Newman, *The Rise of English Nationalism: A Cultural History 1740-1830* (New York: St. Martin's, 1997).

19. J.C.D. Clark, "The Strange Death of British history? Reflections on Anglo-American Scholarship," *The Historical Journal*, 40, 3 (1997), pp. 787-809.

20. Dickens and Carr, *The Reformation in England*, p. 154.

21. Calvin, *Institutes*, I:719-725. Max Weber, *The Protestant Ethic and the Spirit of Capitalism*, trans. T. Parsons, ed. A. Giddens (New York: Routledge, 1992). On Weber, see also William Bouwsma, *John Calvin, a Sixteenth Century Portrait* (New York: Oxford University Press, 1989), pp. 202. Weber argues that Calvin had a distinct notion of the calling. Calvin himself lacked some of the notions that Weber assigned to Calvinism. See Calvin, *Institutes*, note 8, I:724. Bouwsma explains that Calvin and Calvinism differed fundamentally. Like Copernicus, Calvin clung to many medieval ideas and was himself hardly modern, yet his work was a doorway through which others walked into modernity.

22. John A. Taylor, *British Monarchy, English Church Establishment, and Civil Liberty* (Westport, Conn.: Greenwood Press, 1996); and, by the same author, *Popular Literature and the Construction of British National Identity 1707-1850* (San Francisco: International Scholars Publications, 1997).

23. Correlli Barnett, *The Collapse of British Power* (Atlantic Highland, N.J.: Humanities Press, 1986); Warren Hoge, "Blair's Brand-New Britain is No Museum," *New York Times*, 12 November 1997, Midwest Edition; Sidney Pollard, *Britain's Prime and Britain's Decline: the British Economy 1870-1914* (London: Arnold, 1989); Margaret Thatcher, *The Downing Street Years* (New York: Harper Collins, 1993); W.D. Rubinstein, *Culture, Capitalism, and Decline 1750-1990* (London: Routledge, 1993); Martin J. Wiener, *English Culture and the Decline of the Industrial Spirit* (New York: Cambridge University Press, 1981).

24. Vernon Bogdanor, "Sceptred Isle--or Isles?" *Times Literary Supplement*, 4930 (26 September 1997), pp. 4-5.

25. Adam Smith, *The Theory of Moral Sentiments*, ed. D.D. Raphael and A. L. Macfie (Indianapolis: Liberty Classics, 1982), pp. 179-187. The key passage is on pp. 184-5 and is as follows. "The rich only select from the heap what is most precious and agreeable. They consume little more than the poor, and in spite of their natural selfishness and rapacity, though they mean only their own conveniency, though the sole end which they propose from the labours of all the thousands whom they employ, be the gratification of their own vain and insatiable desires, they divide with the poor the produce of all their improvements. They are led by an invisible hand to make nearly the same distribution of the necessaries of life, which would have been made, had the earth been divided into equal portions among all its inhabitants, and thus without intending it, without knowing it, advance the interests of the society."

26. Athol Fitzgibbons, *Adam Smith's System of Liberty, Wealth, and Virtue* (Oxford: Oxford University Press, 1995), p. v.

27. J.S. Mill, *Utilitarianism*, ed. Oscar Piest (New York: Macmillan, 1957), p. 37.

28. Vernon Bogdanor, *The Monarchy and the Constitution* (Oxford: Oxford University Press, 1995), p. 217. Attempting a definitive statement of the present constitutional relationship between the sovereign and the Church of England, Bogdanor wrote, "A church may be defined as a human or divine association composed of those professing a common body of religious doctrine and using common forms of worship." He then went on to say that the state will stand aside "except where it has to intervene to secure certain specific purposes."

TO THE READER

Seeing we are all bound, in the dutiful respect of a common just cause, even to defend those who are strangers to us; it cannot seem unfit to any, if we afford them so much favour, whose persons and deserts are very well known. There is no better contentment for our labour past, than in the assurance from our conscience, that it is well employed: for, doubtless, the spurning at virtue giveth a greater stroke to the doer, than to him that suffereth; and yet even that religion, that commandeth patience, forbiddeth not the just defence of ourselves in a good cause; especially then, when by wronging a particular man, there may be some hazard of the Truth itself. Our church hath had some enemies more openly discontent, in the case of Discipline, than they now appear; whom to satisfy with reason, Master HOOKER endeavoured with much pains: that which might have contented all, was in divers, a spur to a more violent choler: for medicines, how profitable soever, work not equally in all humours. From hence proceedeth a desire in some, to make question of things whereof there was no doubt, and a request for "resolution," of some points, wherein there was no danger: to this end, "a Letter" (which here is answered) was published by "certain Protestants" (as they term themselves), which I hear (how true I know not) is translated into other tongues; this, they presume, hath given that wound to that reverend and learned man, that it was not the least cause to procure his death. But it is far otherwise; for he contemned it in his wisdom (as it was fit) and yet in his humility would have answered it, if he had lived. Surely for mine own part, I never thought it convenient that the gravity of this present business, and the reverend worthiness of him that is accused, should not be answered with gravity both of person and speech; and my witnesses are both in heaven and earth, how justly I can excuse myself, as Elihu did: "Behold, I did wait upon the word of the ancient, and harkened for their knowledge:" "I stayed the time,"* and a long time, until some elder and of riper judgment, might have acquitted me from all opinion of

---

*Job xxxii 11, 16

presumption in this cause; which being not done by them, whom many reasons might have induced to this Defence, I could not for that part which I bear in that Church, whose Government was defended by Master HOOKER, with patience endure so weak a "Letter" any longer to remain unanswered. And herein I have dealt as with men (although to me unknown) of some learning and gravity, to whom peradventure

in many respects I am far inferior; and yet for any thing that I know, or appeareth in this "Letter," they may be clothed with the same infirmities that I am. But if this had been by himself performed (which I hear he hath done, and I desire thee to expect it) thy satisfaction, gentle Reader, would have been much more, yet vouchsafe in thy kindness, to accept this.

W. Covel

---

*Job xxxii. 11, 16

TO THE

MOST REVEREND FATHER IN GOD, MY VERY GOOD LORD,

THE

LORD ARCHBISHOP OF CANTERBURY HIS GRACE,

PRIMATE, AND METROPOLITAN OF ALL ENGLAND.

THREE principal causes, Right Reverend, have moved me to offer this small Labour to your Grace's view: First, the just respect of my particular duty; which challengeth all parts of my labour, as a most thankful acknowledgement of that service which I owe unto you. Secondly, the Form of our Church-Government, which imposeth a submitting of our labours to the censure and allowance of those to whom, by right, that charge belongeth; wherein seeing your authority and care, next unto our dread Sovereign, is, and is to be esteemed, greatest, I desire you to vouchsafe to give that allowance, which your Grace in your wisdom shall think fit. The last reason, is the person of him, who (whilst he lived) was advanced, honoured and esteemed by you; and now being dead, his learning, and sincerity, against the false accusations of others, challengeth a Defence at your Grace's hand: for doubtless it is more right to virtue, to defend the deceased, than to advance those that are living. This, as reason ever expecteth at the hands of virtue; so especially then, when men of worth, of desert, of learning, are mistaken and accused, by those that do want all. I crave to the rest of all your Grace's favours, that this last may be added, That whatsoever my imperfections are, in this Just and Temperate Defence, they may no way diminish the honourable remembrance of him, whom I do defend: all allowance is his due; the faults are mine; for which in all humility, I crave pardon.

Your Grace's to be commanded,

W. Covel

THE AUTHOR'S PREFACE.

Little hath labour done to make any man excellent, if virtue have not as much power to make it continue: neither were it any honour to deserve well, if our memories might die with our names; or our names be buried as often as malice or envy doth seek to hide them. Few things are eminently good which are endured, amongst distempered judgments, without bitter reprehension; for where weakness hath not strength enough to imitate and reverence that virtue which it feareth; it hath violence and malice sufficient to detract from that virtue which it hateth. Amongst evil persons, as there be few things that are good in themselves; so there be not many things which they are willing should appear good in others; for virtue, where it is not followed, must either be dispraised, or our negligence shall want excuse. And whatsoever hath the power to convince, must suffer reproof, where the heart of man wanteth humility to give obedience. The world's greatest error is, in esteeming; when our corruptions making us ambitious to seem, whilst we are careless to be, winneth allowance from a fond opinion, which the stream of violent fancies denieth to rest upon those that are truly virtuous. Because, for any man to oppose himself against that evil which is grown heady, either by custom, or patience, is to hazard much of himself, if he be strong; and, in the opinion of many, undoubtedly to perish, if he be weak. And therefore, as vice hath ever had mo [*more*] that did dislike it, than durst dispraise it; so virtue will ever have mo that are willing to allow it in their judgments, than dare adventure to interpose themselves for the defence of that which they do allow. Jealousy, making those to deprave even the very defence of that which their own judgments did think worthy, and their wishes desired might be defended. For, to do that which every man accounteth his own duty, as it argueth, oftentimes, more strength than courage; so, amongst many, it reapeth little else but an opinion of singularity. From this corrupt fountain, (a fountain poisoned by malicious ignorance) have flowed these bitter, but small streams, which the importunity of some men's commendations (arising out of a blind love) have made for power and greatness, like the red sea, to drown (as they say) Pharaoh and all his host. Let them perish in it without help, beaten down with that hand that striketh from above, who seek to hold Israel a servant in Egypt, or captive in the house of bondage: but let them pass through without harm, who courageously have freed the posterity of Jacob, and led Israel to the land of promise. I doubt not but without a miracle, a man of small stature may go through these waters and not be drowned; yet sometimes the most righteous may say, with David, "the overflowing of ungodliness made me afraid."* Deceit usually covereth with a mask (better than the face) that evil which it desireth should kill unseen and unprevented: but error cannot more easily fall, than when it is built upon such a foundation; nor weaker opinions sooner vanish, than when they are bred, nourished, and supported, only with the strength of fancy. It is of small use in the Church (though a thing practised in all ages) for men over-curiously to labour to remove those stains which, like an impure breath, darken the glass of steel, whilst it is warm, but slide off through their own weakness, having no power to make any deeper impression than only air. Any cloth in a hand of no skill or strength, is able to wipe off with ease, those blots or marks that are stained with no greater force or virtue but a hot breath. But, seeing the reputation that virtue challengeth, and industrious labour, seasoned with discretion, doth merit; seeketh rather to gain an approbation from the judgment of the wise, than recompense or reward from the mighty hand of the rich; men of virtuous desert in all ages, (even from the lowest step of humility and obedience) have, with confidence and truth, taught the world a far better judgment, by their wise apologies; and have gained as much honour in removing evil, as they have gotten virtue unto their names in doing well. The malice of envy, out of impatient ignorance, doing virtue this benefit, That that which was clear before, by a few, light, trifling spots, gaineth a wiping, to make it clearer: *desert* and *goodness*, being effects of a first motion: *perfection* and *excellency* the work of a second maker. It must needs seem strange to many, and be

---

* Psal. xviii. 4.

unpleasing to all that are of any sober, indifferent, or virtuous disposition, that the just Defence of a present, religious, "Ecclesiastical Polity," undertaken without bitterness of spirit, in a grave moderation to reform presumption and inform ignorance, should so far taste of the eagerness of some unlearned pens; that judgement should be thought too weak to answer idle words; or virtue not strong enough to withstand malice; or lastly, that *he* could want a Defence, whose endeavour (as himself professeth) was not so much to overthrow them with whom he contended, as to yield them just and reasonable causes of those things which, for want of due consideration, heretofore they have misconceived; sometimes accusing Laws, for men's oversights; sometimes imputing evils grown through personal defects, to that which is not evil; framing to some sores unwholesome plasters; and applying remedies sometimes where no sores were. It is much easier to answer those shadows of reason wherein A*dmonishers* do please themselves; than, by their silence, to make them confess that they are fully answered. For as they know not (for the most part) well how to speak, saving only tinkers' music, like sounding brass, because they want charity; so do they less know how to hold their peace, like clamorous frogs, because they want humility. Holy pretences have ever been the strongest motives that pride hath; and zeal, how preposterous and ignorant soever, hath been deemed reason sufficient to some men, in the opinion of their followers, to warrant and defend whatsoever they have done. Upon this ground, was published, some few Articles in manner of a "Letter," in the year 1599, "requiring resolution in matters of doctrine," concerning some points, which either they misconceive or list not to understand, uttered by Mr. HOOKER, in those Five learned and grave books of "ECCLESIASTICAL POLITY;" wherein, it must needs appear, that their ignorant malice hath done him great honour; who, in an argument so distasted by them, and coming with a proud confidence to reprehend, have only carped sillily at some few things neither of moment nor importance, whereof humility and charity would have craved no answer. But these being willing and desirous to find somewhat to oppose, have only discovered his great, mature, and grave judgment, and their own small,

and commend a workman, than to see envy desirous to reprehend, and reprehension to vanish in his [*its*] own smoke. For (saith the Wiseman) "all such as regarded not wisdom, had not only this hurt, that they knew not the things that were good; but also left behind them unto men a memorial of their foolishness; so that in the things wherein they sinned, they could not lie hid;"* "yet the people see and understand it not, and consider no such things in their hearts, how that grace and mercy is upon his Saints, and his providence over the elect."† For, as he himself well noted, " as to the best and wisest (while they live) the world is continually a froward opposite, a curious observer of their defects, and imperfections; so their virtues, it afterwards as much admireth." Those, whom we must make adversaries in this cause, are men, not known either by name, religion or learning; yet such as would seem, in zeal to the present State, to desire a "resolution" in some points that might otherwise give offence. It may be, peradventure, the work of some one, who, desirous to gain an opinion amongst his followers, undertaketh to speak as from the minds of many, hoping those demands (how idle soever) will gain answer, being to satisfy a multitude, which no doubt Mr. HOOKER in his wisdom, patience, and gravity, would easily have contemned, if they had but been the private cavils and objections of some one. For there is no man but thinketh *many*, how light so ever in themselves, being united, may have that weight to challenge even by a civil right, a direct answer, from one every way far better than had been fitting for their modesty and weakness to provoke. Well; whosoever they are, as I cannot easily conjecture, so I am not curious to know;* this age hath afforded an infinite number whom superstitious fear for want of true understanding, and an ignorant zeal, not directed with discretion, have made violent in matters of Religion, using the razor instead of a knife, and for hatred of tares oftentimes pulling up good corn. But with these we will deal with that temperate moderation, as may serve to give true worthiness a just Defence; and,

---

* Wisd. x. 8.   † Ibid. iv. 15.   *[Their secret seems to have died with themselves]

impatient and furious spirits (unless desperately violent) no just cause to find themselves to be grieved with us.

This which we are to answer, is termed by them, "A Christian Letter of certain English Protestants, unfeigned favourers of the present state of Religion authorised, and professed in England; unto that Reverend and learned man, Mr. Richard Hooker." Thus the humility and mild temper of their superscription, may peradventure gain the reading at some men's hands, through an opinion that "Protestants," and *many*, and in a "Christian Letter," would hardly be carried with violence so far, to make demands seasoned with so little modesty, learning, or understanding. These men, they may be (as we take the word largely) "Protestants" for any thing that I know; that is, men outwardly of the Christian religion; who live and profess a doctrine, for the most part, opposite to the Church of Rome; but I can hardly be persuaded, that the "Letter" being wholly an uncivil Irony, is either "Christian," or that themselves are "unfeigned favourers of the present state of religion;" or that they think Mr. HOOKER to be either "reverend," or "learned" in their opinions. For, whatsoever they may pretend, in urging the reverend Bishops of our Church against his assertions; as though they ascribed much unto them; yet their desire is, to make an opposition appear, and in that shew of contradiction, to make themselves sport, and in the end proudly and maliciously to contemn both. But St. James telleth these, that "if any man seem religious and refrain not his tongue, but deceiveth his own heart, this man's religion is vain."‡ And in this I appeal to the censure of the most modest and discreet amongst themselves, by what shew of reason they could term that "Letter" to be "Christian" wherein were contained so many unseasoned and intemperate speeches? or, that man to be either "reverend" or "learned," whom they have used with so little respect, and accused of so many defects? But doubtless, as they never thought him to be either "reverend" or "learned" (whom all that knew him whilst he lived knew to be both), so they little

---

‡ James i. 26.

desired that their "Letter" should be such a one as might worthily be accounted "*Christian.*" Else what mean these accusations, to account his "goodly promises mere formal," and "great offers" to "serve only to hoodwink such as mean well;" as though "by excellency of words, and enticing speeches of man's wisdom," he meant, as they say, "to beguile and bewitch the Church of God." A little after, they call him a "goodly Champion," and "by the sweet sound of your melodious style, almost cast into a dreaming sleep;" which style notwithstanding afterwards, they account "not usual," but "long and tedious;" "far differing from the simplicity of holy Scripture;" and a "hard and harsh style:" for the manner of the style, we shall make our defence when we answer that Article. But, in that you scoffingly account him a "goodly Champion," give me leave to tell you that if our Church were thoroughly furnished with such men, the holy function of our calling had not grown in contempt by ignorant and unlearned Ministers; our peace had not been troubled with furious and violent spirits: worldly men had not seized upon the Church with such eagerness, through an opinion of the unworthiness of the Clergy: they of the Church of Rome had not thus long remained obstinate, through the violent proceedings of undiscreet men, whose remedies were worse than the disease itself: nor, last of all, the general amendment of life (the fruit of our preaching) had not been so small, if these turbulent heads had not more desired to make Hypocrites than truly religious. It is much safer to praise the dead than the living, having seen the period of their days expired; "when neither he that is praised can be puffed up, nor he that doth praise can be thought to flatter."§ He was, as St. Austin said of St. Cyprian, "of such desert, of such a courage, of such a grace, of such a virtue,"‖ that as Theodosius said of St. Ambrose, "I have known Ambrose, who alone is worthy to be called a Bishop;" of whom I dare give that judgment (though he were in true estimation great already) which Antigonus gave of Pyrrhus, "that he would have been a *very great* man, if he

---

§ "Quando nec laudantem movet adulatio, nec laudatum tentat elatio."
‖ "Tanti meriti, tanti pectoris, tanti oris, tantæ virtutis."

had been *old*:" Great in his own virtues, of great use in the Church, and in all appearance, (though these times be unthankful) of great authority. I let pass those other terms which shew your "Letter to be un-"Christian," until we come to their particular answers; and thus much for the Title.

*It hath been no new thing, in all ages, that reprehension hath waited upon those Books, which zeal, from a virtuous mind, hath written to support the Truth; for the nature of man is much apter to reprove others than reform itself; seeing, to see faults in others is an act of the understanding, if they be; and of a frowardness of the will, if they be not: but, to rectify them in ourselves must be the work of a clear understanding and a reformed will; therefore usually men practise themselves, what they punish in others; so that no man can directly conclude, That all men hate what they do accuse.† Therefore St. Jerome, of whom saith St. Austin (no man knew that whereof St. Jerome was ignorant) oftentimes complaineth of the detractions, slanders, and untrue accusations of evil men.‡ These, for the most part, are unstaid, violently carried with the current of the present time, sometimes bitterly either upon discontentments, or to please others, inveighing against those, whom themselves before out of flattery, not *judgement*, have highly praised. Thus Libanius the sophister, who was eloquent against the Christians, to please Julian, was noted with this mark of levity, For writing Panegyrics, or orations of praise, to commend Constantius while he lived, against whom afterward he wrote most bitter invectives when he was dead.§ Thus some small discontentment served to turn the heart, and open the mouth of Porphyry against the Christians: what cause of grief these zealous professors have I know not, but in my opinion, the whole tenour of that uncharitable and unchristian "Letter," argueth some inward discontent; either envious that other men should be excellent, or that themselves being excellent, are not more regarded.

---

* The Preface of the Letter answered: "When men dream they are asleep," &c.
† "Ut argumento non sit propter quod alios accusant has ipsas odisse." Dıo. Cass. lib. xxxvi. *Hist.*
‡ Epist. ad Asellam virg. in Prolog. super Jos.
§ Nicephor. Calixtus, lib. x. Host. cap. 36.

Wherein though they dislike the dim eye of government that looketh not clearly into men's virtues, and the niggardly hand that doth not bountifully reward such as deserve well; yet they might out of patience and charity, worthily have forborne to have inveighed against his honour, which consisted in no other wealth but in his religious contentment, and in that true commendation which was the due merit of his own virtues. For the world had not much to take from him, because he had not taken much from the world; for he never affected, flatteringly to please her, nor she never cared fawningly to please him.‖ For as all the Scipio brought from Africa, after his danger and travel, to be called his, was only a surname,* so, the greatest recompense that his labours had was the just commendation, That he was a very reverend, learned and grave man. For his judgment taught him out of a Christian patience, the resolution of Cato, "if I have any thing to use, I use it; if not, I know who I am."† And seeking to profit in knowledge, and that his knowledge might profit the Church; he shewed that he was born for the good of many, and few to be born for the good of him. For as St. Jerome speaketh of Nepotian, "despising gold, he followed learning, the greatest riches." But, peradventure, his learning had puft him up; and his pride had made his writings impatient, and full of bitterness; and this moved you to undertake this uncharitable and unchristian "Letter;" for you say "if we believe them" (meaning the Bishops) "we must think, that Master Hooker is very arrogant and presumptuous, to make himself the only *Rabbi*."§ That you had no cause to provoke him in these terms, all men know that do read his writings; for dealing in an argument of that kind, with adversaries, of that nature; and, in a time grown insolent by sufferance; he hath written with that temperate moderation, rather like a grave father to reform the unstayed errors of hot, young, violent spirits, than severely correcting them with the intemperate bitterness of their own style; and sighing at the

---

‖ Bern. In Obit. Humberti.
* Nihil ex ea quod meum diceretur præter cognomen vetuli." VAL. MAX.
* "Si quid est quo utar, utor; si non, ego sum."
† "Nepotianus noster aurum calcans schedulas consectatus."

scurrilous and more than satirical immodesty of Martinism, he feared with a true
sorrow, lest that honourable calling of Priesthood, which was ruinated by slander
amongst ourselves, could not long continue firm in the opinion of others.‖ Well, for
all this the government of his passions was in his own power,¶ as Saint Bernard
speaketh of Malachy the Bishop. And he was able to rule them; for he was truly of
a mild spirit and an humble heart, and abounding in all other virtues; yet he specially
excelled in the grace of meekness: for the gravity of his looks (as Saint Bernard
speaketh of Humbert), was cleared by those that did sit, or converse with him, lest
he should be burdensome unto them; but a full laughter, few ever discerned in him.**
Some such our Church hath had in all ages; a few now alive, which are her
ornament, if she can use them well; but more that are dead, whom she ought to
praise. For "all those were honourable men in their generations, and were well
reported of, in their times; there are of them, that have left a name behind them, so
that their praise shall be spoken of;" "for whose posterity a good inheritance is
reserved, and their seed is contained in the covenant; their bodies are buried in
peace, but their name liveth for evermore; the people speak of their wisdom, and the
congregation talk of their praise."* In this number virtue hath placed him whom you
accuse: and are not afraid, being now awaked out of a "dream," to account a
deceiver. As though in his labours he had meant by "enticing speech," to deceive the
Church; or as though by a colourable defence of the Church Discipline, he purposed
(as you say) "to make questionable, and to bring in contempt the doctrine and faith
itself; "beating against the heart of all true Christian doctrine, professed by her
Majesty, and the whole State of this realm." Therefore you have made choice of the
principal things contained in his Books; wishing him to free himself "from all
suspicion of falsehood and treachery;" accounting yourselves to rest "contented," if
he will shew himself, either " all one in judgment with the Church of England;" "or

§ Lege Carol. Mag. fol. 421.   ‖ "Ira ejus in manu ejus." BERN.
** "Serenebat vultum suum assidetium gratia, ne fieret onerosus, sed risum integrum si bene
recolitis non admisit." BERN.
* Eccles. xliv, 7, 8, 11-15.

else freely and ingenuously acknowledge his unwilling oversight; or at the least shew plainly by good demonstration, that all our reverend Fathers have hitherto been deceived." To this you crave a "charitable, direct, plain, sincere, and speedy answer;" this is the sum of the Preface to your Christian Letter. It is too true that all ages have had deceivers; and, that the most dangerous deceivers have strongly prevailed under pretence of Religion; and therefore whereas all bodies are subject to dissolution, there are undoubtedly more estates overthrown, through diseases within themselves, which familiarly do steal upon them, than through violence from abroad. Because the manner is always to cast a doubtful and a more suspicious eye, towards that, over which men know they have least power; and therefore the fear of apparent dangers, causeth their forces to be more united; it is to all sorts a kind of bridle; it maketh virtuous minds watchful; it holdeth contrary dispositions in suspense; and employeth the power of all wits; and the wits of all men, with a greater care. Whereas deceits covered with good pretences, are so willingly entertained, so little feared, and so long suffered, until their cruelty burst forth when it is too late to cure them. Vice hath not a better means to disperse itself, nor to gain entertainment and favour, than by borrowing the counterfeit name and habit of seeming virtue. Thus that rebellious Sandracot under pretence of liberty moved the Indians against the officers of Alexander the Great; which when they had slain, he that was the author of their liberty turned that into a more cruel bondage; oppressing the people whom he had freed from strangers, under the cruel tyranny of his own government.* But of all deceits there is none more dangerous, than when the name of God, or Religion, is pretended, to countenance our heinous crimes. And howsoever even in this kind, this age hath not wanted examples, who being dangerous under holy pretences, the hand of Justice hath cut off; yet the imputation of this fault can in no reason cleave to him, who hath so far hazarded himself for the just defence of religion and Church Government. If he had broached any new fancies, or proudly opposed the wise

---

* Justin lib. xv. ex Trogo

established Discipline; there had been some reason to have suspected that by. "enticing speech" he had meant to deceive "the Church." But seeing he hath laboured in a weighty cause, with reasons, against those whom the Magistrate's severity could not easily suppress; seeing he hath undertaken it by appointment; and performed it with allowance; and seeing he hath made no other shew of supporting Popery, but only by resisting Puritans; the slander must needs be too light, and the accusation without colour, to say that he hath "beaten against the heart of all true Christian doctrine, professed by her Majesty and the whole State of this Realm:" as though (which you desire the world might believe) the heart of Christian religion were only among such whom the affectation of singularity hath termed by the name of "Puritans:" And that the rest who are not of that temper, are dangerous and close heretics. Thus Apollinarius the younger, who wrote so much in defence of the Christian faith that St. Basil said of him, that with his volumes he had filled the whole world;† and wrote against raving and frantic Porphyry, thirty books, more excellent than any other of his works: was afterward accused that he held the error of the Millenaries, That into the Trinity he had brought, Great, greater, and greatest of all; that he thought not right of the incarnation of Christ: But seeing Theophilus Bishop of Alexandria, who was an enemy unto him, and divers other authors besides, report that he was vehement to confute the Arians, Eunomians, Origenists, and many other heretics, in many volumes, it may be thought whatsoever his other errors were, the malice of his adversaries had forged this, to diminish the authority of those books which he had written against them.‡ So that this practice is no new thing, To diminish the soundness of their religion whose judgments and reasons we are unable to withstand. But I doubt not by that which followeth, but it shall easily be made to appear that he is of the same judgment with the Church of England: that he hath not committed any oversight; nor that he goeth not about to contradict, "the reverend fathers of our Church:" which things (in all likelihood) are matters by all you much

---

† Sixt. Sin. lib. iv. Bibliothecæ.   ‡ Epiphanius in 3. Pannarii.
* Justin. lib. xv. ex Trogo

desired; and therefore I hope you will accept (as you desire) *this* "charitable, direct, plain, and sincere Answer;" which no doubt of it, from himself had been far more learned and more speedy if he could either have resolved to have done it, or after he had resolved could have lived to have seen it finished. But first of all, he was loth to inter-meddle with so weak adversaries; thinking it "unfit" (as himself said) "that a man that hath a long journey, should turn back to beat every barking cur;" and having taken it in hand, his urgent and greater affairs, together with the want of strength, weakened with much labour, would not give him time to see it finished. Yet "his mind was stronger than his years, and knew not well how to yield to infirmity."* Wherein if he had somewhat favoured himself, he might peradventure, have lived to have answered you; to the benefit of the Church, and the comfort of a great number. But "death hath done what he could; it hath killed his body, and it is laid up in the heart of the earth; it hath taken from us, and from the church of God, a sweet friend, a wise counsellor, and a strong champion:"† so that I may say, as it was sometimes said of Demosthenes: "Demosthenes is meet for Athens, Demades overgreat." Others fit enough to live in the midst of error, vanity, unthankfulness, and deceit, but he too good. For "he was as the Morning Star in the midst of a cloud, and as the Moon when it is full; and as the Sun shining upon the Temple of the most High, and as the Rainbow that is bright in the fair clouds;" "when he put on the garment of honour, and was clothed with all beauty, he went up to the holy Altar; and made the garment of holiness honourable."‡ But this ought to content us, "That the souls of the righteous are in the hand of God, and no torment shall touch them: In the sight of the unwise they appeared to die, and their end was thought grievous, and their departing from us destruction; but they are in peace."§

---

* "Erat animus victor annorum, et cedere nesciens infirmitati." BERN. *in Vita Humberti.*
† "Mors fecit quantum potuit, occidit carnem, et ecce recondita est in corde terræ; separavit à nobis dulcem amicum, prudentem Consiliarium, Auxiliarium fortem." BERN.
‡ Eccles.1. 6, 7, 11.   § Wisd. iii. 1-3.

THE ARTICLES HANDLED IN THIS BOOK

THE
DEFENCE

ARTICLE I.

OF THE DEITY OF THE SON OF GOD

All points in Divinity are not of the like easiness of apprehension. For in some, the dim light of nature, not wholly darkened, can give a reason of that we do; as well as faith, out of precept, doth warrant what we do believe. And therefore the Gentiles both before and after the Law, were to themselves a kind of Law, even by the light of nature, not to do all those things that they did desire; but they had a thing in their hearts, equivalent to the Law in respect of forbidding, because they could accuse and excuse themselves, having the witness of their conscience present with them.* Thus the effect of all the Commandments, was in the Jews before the Law, and in the Gentiles who had not the Law, given unto them. Thus the first commandment was in Terah, Abraham's father; which was the reason of his departure from Ur of the Chaldees, to go into the land of Canaan.† And afterwards in Jacob, when he departed out of Laban's house; above four hundred years before the law was given:‡ so the second commandment in Rachel;§ the third, in Abraham to his servant:‖ the fourth, had a precept in the creation: the fifth, for honouring his parents, even in Essau:¶ the sixth, in Cain, who knew the greatness of that evil which he had committed, that slew his brother; fear making him out of a guilty conscience,

---

* [Rom. ii. 12-15.]   † Gen. xi. 31.   ‡ *Ibid.* xxxi. 3.
§ Gen. xxxi. 34.   ‖ Ibid. xxiv. 3.   ¶ *Ibid.* xxvii. 41

2

to deny that, which love before had not power enough to teach him to forbear.* The seventh, in the hatred of the sin of Sichem; which Jacob, though he allowed not to be rightly punished, yet he did not approve as to be well done.† The eighth, even in Egypt, which made Joseph to say, What act is that you have done? when the cup of Pharaoh was found in the sack of Benjamin.‡ The ninth, when Judah feared the witness of Thamar.** The last, in Abimelech for taking the wife of Abraham, where the vision did not so much tell him it was a sin, (which he knew by nature) as that she was another man's wife.†† Now in these things which were observed before the Moral Law, some were of more apparent dislike, even in the opinion of the heathen, who had no other direction but the light of nature; as the third, fifth, sixth, seventh, eighth, and ninth commandments. For the Egyptians had a Law; "Swear not, lest thou die."‡‡ And this was punished in the twelve tables of the Romans.§ For the fifth, Homer saith of one that had a misfortune, "it was because he honoured not his parents." For the sixth, nature hath made the murderer to expect what he hath committed. ‖ For the seventh, Flee the name of an adulterer, if thou wilt escape death.¶ For the eighth, Demosthenes against Timocrates repeateth it as Solon's Law, plainly in the very words.*** And for false witness, the Romans did punish it by their twelve tables.††† But the incarnation of Christ, the Sacraments, the Trinity, the Decree of God, are matters of a deeper speculation; wherein humility must follow the direction of Faith, and not seek vainly with curiosity to know that, which our silly weakness is far unable to comprehend. For, as those things that are manifest are not to be neglected, so those things that are hid, are not to be searched; lest in the one we be unlawfully curious, and in the other be found dangerously unthankful.‡‡ Now

---

.* *Ibid.* iv. 9.   † *Ibid.* xxxiv. 31; xlix. 6.   ‡‡ *Ibid.* xliv 12, 15.
** Gen. xxxviii. 23.   †† *Ibid.* xx. 3.   ‡‡ Diodorus Sicul.   § Fustibus cæditur
‖ Homicida quod fecit expectat.   ¶ Fuge nomen mæchi si mortem fugies.
* * Stephanus ex Nicostrato.   †† Tarpeio Saxo dejiciatur. Leg. 12. Tabul.
‡‡ "Quæ deus occulta esse voluit, non sunt scrutanda; quæ autem manifesta fecit, non sunt negligenda; ne et in illis illicite curiosi, et in his damnabiliter inveniantur ingrati." PROSPER. *de vocat Gentium.*.

specially for the matter of the Trinity, wherein you take exception in your two first Articles; doubtless there are few errors more dangerous, or that have stirred up greater tragedies in the church of God.§§ All men see in nature, that there is a God; but the distinction of persons, Trinity in Unity, that, Faith, in humility, must teach us to believe. For who can comprehend by reason, that in that holy and sacred Trinity, one is what three are, and that two is but one thing; and in themselves and every particular infinite; and all in every one, and every one in all, and all in all, and one in all. Fire hath three things, motion, light, and heat: Arius, divide this if thou canst, and then divide the Trinity? Out of this difficulty, together with the rash presumption of ignorant men, have proceeded those dangerous errors, that so long and so hotly have troubled the Church: thus the Manichies have denied the unity of Essence; the Valentinians (or Gnostics) from Carpocrates, held that Christ was man only, from both sexes born; but that he had such a soul, which knew all things that were above, and shewed them.* Those that have in their erroneous doctrine oppugned the Trinity, are of two sorts; they have either denied the distinction of Persons, or else the sameness of Essence: thus the Arians (for we will not stand to encounter or confute all other heresies) held that Christ was a person before his incarnation; but that he was true and eternal God, equal and of the same essence with his Father, that they denied; for they hold that the Son is not eternally begotten of the substance of his Father, and so that there is an inequality, and indeed a distinction, and priority of essence. Into this dangerous and ignorant blind heresy, confuted long since with powerful and strong reasons, it seems you are of opinion that Master HOOKER is fallen, both against the truth and against the true assertions of the Reverend Fathers of our church. The ground of this so great and so uncharitable accusation, is because he saith, that "The Father alone is originally that Deity which *Christ originally* is not." Where you seem to infer, against the distinction of the Trinity, that the

---

§ "Nec periculosius alicubi erratur, nec laboriosius aliquid quæritur, nec fructuosius aliquid invenitur." AUG. lib. iv. *de Trinitat.*
* Aug. Tom. VI. Ser. 7.

4

Godhead of the Father and the Son cannot be all one, if the Son be not originally that Deity. It seems then in your opinions, that this speech uttered very learnedly, and with great wisdom, and truth; "The Father alone is originally that Deity which Christ originally is not," is both unusual, new, and dangerous. First, because it weakeneth "the eternity of the Son, in the opinion of the simple, or maketh the Son inferior to the Father in respect of the Godhead, or else teacheth the ignorant that there may be many Gods." I know your own Christian judgments could easily have freed him from all suspicion of error in this point, if your charity had been equal to your understanding: for he himself hath confessed in the very same place from whence you have taken this whereof you accuse him; that "By the gift of eternal generation, Christ hath received of the Father one, and in number the selfsame substance, which the Father hath of himself unreceived from any other." Who seeth not, saith St. Augustine, that these words, Father, and Son, shew not the diversities of natures, but the relation of persons; and therefore the Son is not of another nature and of a divers substance, because the Father is God, not from another God, but the Son is God from God his Father: "here is not declared the substance but the original; that is, not what he is, but from whence he is, or is not:"§ for in God the Father, and in God the Son, if we inquire the nature of them both, both are God, and but one God, neither greater nor less in essence of Godhead, one than the other. But if we speak of the original, saith St. Austin (which you see Master Hooker did) the Father is God originally, from whom the Son is God; but there is not from whom the Father hath originally his deity. So that to mislike this kind of speech is, contrary to all truth, to affirm, that the Son is not eternally begotten of the Father, and that the Father is not eternally a deity begetting. But here you must take heed of the error of Arius, who against the truth reasoned thus; If the Son be co-eternal with his Father, tell us, we beseech you, whether he were begotten when he was, or when he was not; if when he was, then

---

§ "Hic non indicatur substantia, sed origo, id est, non quid sit, sed unde sit, vel non sit." AUG. Epist. 66. *ad Maxim*

there was before two unbegotten, and afterwards one begot the other; if when he was not, then he must needs be later, and after his Father. But saith St. Augustine, as we have known only the Father always and without beginning to be unbegotten; so we confess, the Son always and without beginning to be begotten of his Father: therefore, because the Father is originally that Deity, from whence the Son is the Son; though he be the same Deity, yet the Father alone, is originally that Deity, which the Son originally is not. The want of Identity being not in the Deity (whereof we must needs with the Church of God acknowledge an Unity) but in that it is not originally the same. "For every thing that is a beginning, is a father unto that which cometh of it, and every offspring is a son unto that out of which it groweth." "Christ then being God, by being of God, light by issuing out of light," though he be the same deity (for in the Trinity there is but one deity) yet the Father is originally that Deity alone, which Christ originally is not. Here, if you note but the difference betwixt that "Deity," and "originally that Deity," you must needs confess that Mr. Hooker speaketh with the consent of reformed antiquity, and hath said nothing to diminish the eternity of the Son, or to make him inferior, in respect of his Father; or to teach the ignorant, that there be many Gods.

ARTICLE II.

THE CO-ETERNITY OF THE SON, AND THE PROCEEDING OF THE HOLY GHOST

In this Article, the thing which you mislike is not any matter of his judgment, but that he seemeth to confess, either out of less learning than you have or more humility than you shew, that "the co-eternity of the Son of God with his Father, and the proceeding of the Spirit from the Father and the Son, are in Scripture no where to be found by express literal mention:" and yet you cannot be ignorant, but that undoubtedly he believed both. Therefore, in my opinion, it is strange, why, out of the Second and Fifth Article holden by our Church, you allege, that "The Son is the Word of the Father, from everlasting begotten of the Father;" and, "The Holy Ghost proceeding from the Father and the Son;" as though you dealt with an adversary that denied either. You could not be ignorant (having perused his writings with that diligence to reprehend), but in this great mystery of the Trinity,–both concerning the equality of the Son with the Father, and the Deity of the Holy Ghost who proceedeth from both,–see plainly that he held directly and soundly that doctrine which is most true, and every way agreeable with the judgments and expositions of the Reverend Fathers of our Church. Neither do I know whether, in this point, any of them have left behind them a more sound, learned, and virtuous Confession, than he hath done. For, saith he; "The Lord our God is but one God. In which indivisible unity, notwithstanding, we adore the Father, as being altogether of himself; we glorify that

8

consubstantial Word, which is the Son; we bless and magnify that co-essential Spirit eternally proceeding from both, which is the Holy Ghost."* What confession can there be, in this point, of greater judgment, learning, and truth? and wherein there is less difference with that which our Church holdeth? both having their ground, as you may see by the places alleged by Mr. Hooker in the margin, from the infallible evidence of God's Word. This troubleth you, that he saith, that these points "are in Scripture no where to be found, *by express literal mention:*" which you, out of your learned observation, have proved (as you think) to be far otherwise, by those places of Scripture, which his careless reading and weak judgment, was no way able to observe! Where, first, to prove the co-eternity of the Son, you allege, "The Lord hath possessed me in the beginning of his way; I was before his works of old." And again, "In the beginning was the Word, and the Word was with God, and the Word was God."† And again, "Glorify me, thou Father, with thine own self, with the glory which I had with thee before the world was."‡ These places I confess, by way of collection, may serve, truly to confirm in this Article, that which our Church holdeth; (and yet they are not the plainest places that might be alleged for this purpose). But in all these, where is there to be found "express literal mention," of the "co-eternity" of the Son, with the Father? Nay, for any thing that ever I could read, I do not think you are able to find the word co-eternal, or co-equal, in the whole Scripture in this sense. For after the Arians had long in this point troubled the Church, the holy Fathers express what they held, by the word "Homousion;" which word St. Augustine affirmeth, not to be found in all the Scripture.§ What then hath Master Hooker said; which St. Augustine said not long since? neither of them disproving the thing, but both denying the "express literal mention" of the word; which I persuade myself yourselves are never able to find.

---

* Prov. viii. 22.   † John i. 1.   ‡ John xvii._
§ Aug. Tom. II. epist. 174.

Now, for "the proceeding of the Holy Ghost," you allege, as you say, express words: "When the Comforter shall come, whom I will send unto you from the Father, even the Spirit of truth, which proceedeth of the Father"‖ Out of this place (as you think) you have sufficiently proved, the "express literal mention" of this point: we contend not with you, nor with any, Whether the truth of this point may directly be warranted by holy Scripture; but, Whether there be, as you say, "express literal mention." First then we call that "express literal mention," which is set down in plain terms, and not inferred by way of consequence: that it is so in this point, we have some reason to doubt until, out of your great observation, you confirm it by more plain and apparent Scripture. For against this place (which is but one) which you have alleged, we take this twofold exception; as thereby accounting it insufficient to prove, as you would have it, that there is "express literal mention" of the proceeding, of the Spirit from the Father and the Son. For first, in that place alleged out of St. John, there is no mention at all of proceeding from the Son. Secondly, as Master Beza (whose authority you will not deny) doth expound the place, Christ speaketh not of the essence of the Holy Ghost in himself, but of the virtue and power of the Holy Ghost in us:* neither doth his interpretation (which we will not examine at this time) any way prejudice the foundation of that truth, which our Church doth hold. For the Deity of the Holy Ghost proceeding from the Father, and the Son, though not by any "express literal mention," yet may easily be proved by infinite places of Scripture, and other infallible demonstrations besides this. In the days of Liberius the Pope, and of Constantius the Emperor, certain fantastical spirits held, That the Holy Ghost was not God; but only the ministerial instrument of divine working. This began under Arius, and increased by Eunomius, a leprous heretic, but a subtile Logician; whom the Church hath strongly confuted, with arguments impossible to be answered. As first, that the Holy Ghost is every where; to give all things: to know and search all things;† that we are commanded to baptize"

‖ John xv. 26   * In Comment. in Johan. xv. 26.   † Psal. cxxvi. 1 Cor. ii. 10. James i.

10

in the name of the Father, of the Son, and of the Holy Ghost:"‡ besides the greatness
of the sin against the Holy Ghost:§ So Ananias that lied, as Peter said, " to the Holy
Ghost, lied not to man, but to God."‖ These and many such places, warranted those
ancient Councils to conclude the Deity of the Holy Ghost, equal to the Father and the
Son; and equally proceeding from both. As first, the Council of Constantinople,
consisting of an hundred and fifty Bishops, under Theodosius the elder, and Damasus
the Pope, which condemned the heresy of the Macedonians.¶ The same faith was
confirmed by the Council of Ephesus; the Council of Chalcedon;** the Council of
Lateran, under Innocentius the Third,† and divers others. And Athanasius himself
maketh it most plain, That the Father is of none, either made, created, or begotten:
the Son is of the Father alone, not made, nor created, but begotten: the Holy Ghost
is from the Father, and the Son, not made, nor created, nor begotten, but proceeding.
In this, nothing being first, or last, greater, or less; but all the three persons, co-eternal
and co-equal. The proceeding of the Holy Ghost (as the Schoolmen observe) is
three-fold; one, unspeakable and eternal, whereby the Holy Ghost eternally, and
without time, proceedeth from the Father and the Son; the other, temporal, when he
is sent from the Father and the Son, to sanctify the elect. Of this latter proceeding
saith Beza, is that place understood,–which you peremptorily allege, for to prove the
first. So then we say, for our answer to this cavil, That as yet we see not "express
literal mention" of these points; but that they are truly and soundly collected by the
Church, we neither do, can, nor dare deny; secondly, That the denial of "express
literal mention," ought not to make any scruple in the minds of weak Christians,
concerning these articles, the substance whereof are plain Scripture; though for the
words we find not as yet any "express literal mention:" nor, last of all, (as you seem
to fear) it can be no *underpropping* to the "traditions" of the Church of Rome; which
if they can prove with the like necessary collection out of the holy Scripture, we are

---

‡ Matt. xxviii. 20.   § Matt xii. 31.   ‖ [Acts v. 3.]
¶ About the year 381   ** 430   †† 451

ready to embrace them with all our hearts. In the mean time, we account it a wrong to have an article of our faith, for want of "express literal mention" out of Scripture, to be compared to traditions of that kind, for which in Scripture there is no warrant at all. To conclude, then, this article, we say, That in the Trinity there is that Identity of essence–that is admitteth equality, but not plurality: the Father is one, the Son another, the Holy Ghost another, but not another thing. * For that thing that they all are is the one thing, that they are one God. So that St. Austin saith, "I and my Father are one;" here both the words of the sentence, "one," and "are,"–in that he saith "one," he freeth thee from Arius; and in that he saith "are," he freeth thee from Sabellius.† For "are," he would not say of one; and "one," he would not say of divers: for every person hath his own substance, which no other besides hath, although there be others besides which are of the same substance. For "the Persons of the Godhead, by reason of the unity of their substance, do as necessarily remain one within another, as they are of necessity to be distinguished one from another: because two are the issue of one; and one, the offspring of the other two; only of three, one, not growing out of any other. For sith they all are but one God in number, one indivisible essence or substance, their distinction cannot possibly admit separation;.....the Father therefore is in the Son, and the Son in him; they both in the Spirit, and the Spirit in both them:" He that can, saith Austin, conceive, let him comprehend it, but he that cannot, let him believe, and pray that that which he believeth, he may truly understand.§

---

* Aug. in Psal. lxviii. Alius non aliud. Unum non unus.
† Aug. Tom. IX. in Evang. Job. tract. 36. Damasc. de Orthodox. Fid. lib. iii. cap. 6.
§ Aug. Tom. VI. cont. Max. lib. iii. epist. 10.

ARTICLE III.

WHETHER THE HOLY SCRIPTURES CONTAIN ALL THINGS NECESSARY TO SALVATION?

Two things are requisite to man's better life; a Faith to believe what he ought, a Knowledge to comprehend what he must believe. For, saith our Saviour, in "this is eternal life, to know thee to be the only very God; and whom thou hast sent, Jesus Christ." Because, therefore, the want of this knowledge is the cause of all iniquity amongst men; as, contrariwise, the very ground of all our happiness, and the seed of whatsoever perfect virtue groweth from us, is a right opinion touching things divine; this kind of knowledge we may justly set down, for the first and chiefest thing which God imparteth to his people; and, our duty of receiving this at his merciful hands, for the first of those religious offices wherewith we publicly honour him on earth. Now our Church holdeth, and we most willingly confess, that the Scripture is the true ground of all that holily we believe. But yet for all that, not the only means, concerning God, of all that profitably we know. For that new impression, made into our nature, even by the hand of the Almighty, after the first sin; and the wise beholding of his excellent workmanship, in the making of all his creatures, are two volumes wherein we may read (though not directly) the mercy of that power, that hath saved us; yet, the greatness, and the might of that hand that hath first made us: which though it be not all that we must believe, yet it is not the least part of that which we ought to know. For this, as it maketh us without excuse, so it serveth even to lead us to a better knowledge: and (until it be perfect) to utter out of the light of

14

nature,† those voices, which may argue us, though not to be sons (for by this we cannot cannot cry "Abba, Father") yet to be reasonable creatures of that power which we do adore; this made Euripides in Troas, and many of the heathen, to utter those prayers, which had they been offered up in Christ, had not been unbeseeming a good Christian: so that though "the Scriptures contain all things, which are necessary to salvation;" and that "our chiefest direction," is from them; yet we are not afraid to confess, that there is besides a "light of Nature" not altogether unprofitable; the insufficiency whereof is, by the light of Scripture, fully and perfectly supplied: and that both these together, as Master Hooker affirmeth, which you mislike, " do serve in such full sort, that they both jointly, and not severally either of them, be so complete, that unto everlasting felicity we need not the knowledge of any thing more than of these two; I cannot but marvel that men endowed with reason should find any thing in this assertion, which, in the hardest construction, might be wrested as detracting from the sufficiency of the holy Scripture: And only for this cause, by reason that we read darkly, by "the light of Nature," those first elements out of a natural knowledge, which, by the access of a better teacher, serve afterward for the full perfecting of that knowledge which is requisite to man's salvation. For, as the Schoolmen say, man standeth in need of a threefold Law, to a moral uprightness, setting aside that righteousness requisite for his heavenly country. First, an eternal Law (which St. Austin calleth "the chiefest reason"§); secondly, natural; last of all, human; unto which, if we add that man, over and besides these, is in an ordination to a supernatural end,‡ then it is manifest, that to make him a heavenly Citizen there is requisite a fourth Law, which man must learn to obey, out of the holy Scripture. But as in the greatest and fairest buildings, even those stones that lie lowest are of an use not be contemned; though peradventure, not comparable to those last, exquisite,

---

† "O terræ vehiculum, et in terrasedem habens. Quisquis tandem es inaccesse nostris animis Jupiter; sive naturæ ordo sic ferat, sive mens mortalium te venerer: omnia enim secrete, et sine strepitu qui facis incedere via, et justo libramine mortalia et humana." EURIP. *in Troas.*
§ "Summam rationem." *De Libero. Arbit.* lib. i. cap. 6.
‡ Cajetan. ad summam Aquinatis, in quest. 9. 2.

perfections, by which the work is finished; so even "the light of Nature," for the acting of moral virtues, hath his [*its*] use, though not absolutely complete, to make us Christians. And, therefore, in the nature of man's will, the very Philosophers did seldom err; but in the strength of it, often. So that some ascribed more than was fit; others less than they ought; imputing all to a stoical and fatal Necessity. Now that we may truly understand (the ignorance or mistaking whereof, hath been the ground of your exception in this Third article), what good things man of himself may do or know without the grace of God; we are taught first, That all actions are of three sorts; Natural, which are common to man with the brute beasts; as to eat, sleep, and such like, which appertain to his natural life: Secondly, Civil, which we call political, or moral, human actions; as to buy, sell, to learn any art, and to conclude any other action, which concerneth the politic, or private society of man: Thirdly, those which belong to the kingdom of God; to a perfect, happy, and true Christian life; as, to repent us of our sins, to believe in God, to call upon him, to obey his voice, to live after his precepts, and such like: now the question is, What grace and power is requisite to man, to perform any, or all these? Where we must observe, that some men (how properly I know not) make the grace of God to be threefold. First that general motion and action divine, of which Saint Paul saith, "in him we live, we move, and have our being."* This the Schoolmen call a "general overflowing;"† and of the late writers, especially of Luther, it is called "the action of the omnipotency;" and this grace is common to all, that are within that compass to be called creatures. Secondly, there is a grace of God, which is a special favour of God, by the which he bestoweth and divideth his gifts and moral virtues, both to the faithful and unfaithful, as pleaseth him.‡ To the faithful, that having the help afterward of a better light, they may serve to be means of their salvation; to the unfaithful, for special uses, and manifold, in the society of man, and to make themselves, in the end without excuse. Such were those gifts in the Romans and others of the heathen, of justice, fortitude,

---

* Acts xvii. 28.   † Superfluxus generalis.   ‡ 1 Cor. xii. 11.

16

temperance, prudence, which they thought, were from nature; but we acknowledge to be from the special favour of God: for as Being, so Truth is but one, and by whomsoever it is done, or spoken, it proceedeth from the Holy Ghost;§ and therefore I both marvel at those, who make an opposition betwixt this light of nature and the Scripture; being both from one fountain, though running in divers streams; and that some men peevishly refuse the excellentest truths of heathen learning, seeing even in them, these have proceeded from the Holy Ghost.‖ Thirdly, there is a grace of regeneration, or the grace of Christ, without which, there can be nothing performed of man truly good; for saith our Saviour, "Without me, you can do nothing;"¶ and St. Paul, "Not I, but the grace of God which is with me;"** so that this must be the perfection of the other two, which is powerful to man's salvation, not razing out that which before was, but finishing that which before was imperfect. The two first, enduing man with a "passive power" (as the Schoolmen call it), which though actually it can do nothing, yet it is fit to perform that which it hath no repugnancy in his [its] own nature to resist; as wood can be made fire, which water cannot. The last only affording that actual power, which maketh him capable of the supernatural work; so that it is true in divinity, that "The possibility to have faith, is from nature; but to have it, it is of grace," (as St. Austin and Prosper hold;)* neither of them understanding an actual having of faith without the grace of regeneration. This made the Fathers, in their sermons to the people, to stir them up to prayer and good works; to tell them often, that we can love God, and do good works; whereunto they only meant that we had a "passive power," which stocks and brute beasts have not. Now for the *active* power, we hold, That man hath not this in natural things, without the general help of God; and in moral actions, or the learning of arts, not with that general help only (which hath been some men's error), but from a more special and

---

§ "Veritas a quocunque dicatur a Spiritu Sancto est." AMBROS.
‖ "Si unicum veritatis fontem Dei spiritum esse reputamus, veritatem ipsam neque respuemus neque contemnamus ubicunque apparebit." CALVIN. *Inst.* lib. ii. cap. 2. sect. 15.
    ¶ John xv. 5.   ** 1 Cor. xv. 10.
* Posse haabere fidem, est naturæ; habere, gratiæ." AUST. *et* PROSP. *cont. Cassianum.*

peculiar grace: the weakness of those common notions of good and evil, just and unjust, left in our nature by a new impression, after sin, is for the most part such, that they can hardly discern any thing, no not in arts, unless they be enlightened from above. And therefore, that Numa amongst the Romans; Solon amongst the Athenians; Lycurgus amongst the Lacedemonians; and that many other amongst the Gentiles, were wise, and in that kind virtuous; was not so much from nature, as from a special grace: whose moral works saith St. Austin, "were good in their office and action, but not in their end."† This argument he very learnedly handleth, against Julian the Pelagian, where he concludeth two things; That there can be no true virtues, or truly chaste works in Infidels; and, That those works whatsoever they are, are not from nature, but from a special grace. The having whereof, though it serve not of itself to salvation, yet we are not afraid to affirm, that the want of these do ordinarily exclude from salvation: Justice, fortitude, temperance, and prudence, being the effects of the same grace, but less powerfully working; faith, hope, and charity, only taught by a supernatural truth. So that though "the light of nature," teach a truth necessary to salvation, without the Scripture, yet it teacheth no knowledge, which is not contained in holy Scripture; the difference only being in this, That "the light of nature," doth not teach all that the Scripture doth; but that the Scripture teacheth all (and more perfectly) which is taught by "the light of nature:" herein only neither excluded as unnecessary; the one, being subordinate to the other; and both, means of the same thing. To conclude then this point; we hold (being warranted by holy Truth,) That the Scriptures are the perfect measure and rule of faith; and, that without Christ, we cannot be complete;‡ and yet for all this, that nature, so enlightened, teacheth those moral virtues, without which, is no ordinary salvation; but we say not, That matters and cases of salvation be determined by any other law, than warranted by holy Scripture; or that we are or can be justified, by any

---

† "Officio et actione bona sunt, sed non fine." AUST. Tom. VII. lib. iv. cap. 3.
‡ Deut. iv. 2. Gal. i. 8. John xx. *ult.* 2 tim. iii. 16. Rom. x. 17; xv. 4. Eph. ii. 20.

other than in Christ, "by faith without the works of the law:"* "for there is no other name, which is given under heaven, amongst men, by which we must be saved."†
"The natural man perceiveth not the things of the Spirit of God; for they are foolishness unto him:"‡ for "except a man be born again, he cannot see the kingdom of heaven."§

---

* Rom. iii. 28.   † [Acts iv. 12.]   ‡ 1 Cor. ii. 14.   § John iii. 3.

ARTICLE IV.

HOLY SCRIPTURES ABOVE THE CHURCH

Though the unthankfulness of man be without excuse, even from the *brightness* that riseth from looking upon all the Creatures; which with their beams shineth into the darkest corners of man's heart, yet in His mercy, he hath not left him altogether destitute of a better guide. The first, serving to teach him, that there is a God; the latter, what that God is, and how he will be worshipped by man. This *light* we call the Scripture; which God hath not vouchsafed to all, but to those only whom he gathereth more nearly and familiarly to himself, and vouchsafeth that honour to be called his Church; that, as men through infirmity seeing weakly, provide unto themselves, the help of a better sight; so, what man cannot read, by the dimness of his seeing, out of the Creatures, he may more apparently read them, in the holy Scriptures. For as there is no salvation without religion; no religion without faith; so there is no faith without a promise, nor promise without a Word: for God, desirous to make an union betwixt us and himself, hath so linked his Word and his Church, that neither can stand where both are not. The Church for her part, in her choice allowance, testifying, as well that it is the Scripture; as the Scripture, from an absolute authority, doth assure us that it is the Church. For as those who are converted, have no reason to believe that to be the Church, where there is no Scripture; so those who are not converted, have no great reason to admit that for Scripture, for which they have not the Church's warrant. So that, in my opinion, the

20

contention is unnatural and unfit, to make a variance, by comparison, betwixt those two who are, in reason and nature, to support each other. It was a memorable atonement that Abraham made with Lot, "Let there be no strife, I pray thee, between thee and me, neither between thy herdsmen and my herdsmen, for we be brethren;"* so, undoubtedly, may the Church and the Scripture say: it is, then, to be feared that those who treacherously make this contentious comparison betwixt both, are, in very deed, true friends to neither. For though we dislike of them by whom too much, heretofore, hath been attributed to the Church; yet we are loath to grow to an error on the contrary hand, and to derogate too much from the Church of God: by which removal of one extremity with another, the world, seeking to procure a remedy, hath purchased a mere exchange of the evil, which before was felt. We and our adversaries confess, that the Scriptures in themselves have great authority; inward witness from that Spirit, which is the author of all Truth; and outward arguments, strong motives of belief, which cleaveth firmly to the Word itself. For what doctrine was ever delivered with greater majesty? What style ever had such simplicity, purity, divinity? What history, or memorial of learning, is of like antiquity? What oracles, foretold, have been effected with such certainty?† What miracles, more powerful to confirm the truth? What enemies ever prevailed less or laboured more violently to root it out? To conclude, What witnesses have died with more innocency or less fear, than those that have sealed the holiness of this Truth? This the Scripture is, in itself; but men who are of less learning, than these Reformers are, do not unworthily make question, How that which ought thus highly to be esteemed for itself, cometh to be accounted of thus honourably by us; for the weakness of man's judgment doth not ever value things by that worth which they do deserve. For, undoubtedly, out of that error hath proceeded your suspicion of him, whose inward worthiness must now be content to receive testimony from a witness by many thousand degrees inferior to himself. To them of Samaria the woman gave testimony of our Saviour Christ;‡ not

*Gen. xiii. 8.   †1 Kings xiii. 2. Isai. xliv. 28; xlv. 1.   ‡ John iv. 39.

that she was better, but better known; for witnesses of less credit, than those of whom they bear witness, but of some more knowledge than those to whom they bear witness, have ever been reputed to give a kind or warrant and authority unto that they prove. Seeing then the Church, which consisteth of many, doth outwardly testify what every man inwardly should be; to swerve unnecessarily from the judgment of the whole Church, experience as yet hath never found it safe. For that which by her ecclesiastical authority she shall probably think and define to be true, or good, must, in congruity of reason, overrule all other inferior judgments whatsoever. And to them (that out of a singularity of their own) ask us Why we thus hang our judgments on the Church's sleeve? we answer with Solomon, " Two are better than one;§ for even in matters of less moment, it was never thought safe, to neglect the judgment of many, and rashly to follow the fancy and opinion of some few. If the Fathers of our Church had had no greater reason to avouch their forsaking of the "Antichristian Synagogue," (as you call it) than this point; we might justly have wished to have been reconciled to the fellowship and society of their Church. For this point, as it seemeth rightly understood, affordeth little difference betwixt them and us; and therefore there was no mention of it in the last Council their Church had.* And Bellarmine himself doth, apparently, complain, that we wrong them in this point; for doubtless it is a tolerable opinion of the Church of Rome, if they go no further (as some of them do not) to affirm that the Scriptures are holy and divine in themselves, but so esteemed by us for the authority of the Church; for there is no man doubteth but that it belongeth to the Church (if we understand as we ought those truly who are the Church) to approve the Scriptures, to acknowledge, to receive, to publish, and to commend unto her children. And this witness ought to be received of all as true, yet we do not believe the Scriptures for this only; for there is the testimony of the Holy Ghost, without which the commendation of the Church were of little value. That the Scriptures are true to us, we have it from the Church; but that we believe them as

§ Eccles.iv. 9.   * Of Trent.   † Dr. Whitaker.

22

true, we have it from the Holy Ghost.† We confess it is an excellent office of the Church, to bear witness to the Scriptures; but we say not, that otherwise we would not believe them. We grant that the Scriptures rightly used, are the judge of controversies; that they are the trial of the Church; that they are in themselves a sufficient witness for what they are: but yet for all this, we are not afraid, with Master Hooker, to confess, that "it is not the Word of God which doth or possibly can assure us, that we do well to think it is the Word of God." For "by experience we all know, that the first outward motion leading men so to esteem of the Scripture, is the authority of God's Church," which teacheth us to receive Mark's Gospel, who was not an apostle, and refuse the Gospel of Thomas who was an Apostle, and to retain St. Luke's Gospel, who saw not Christ, and to reject the Gospel of Nicodemus that saw him. For though, in themselves, they have an apparent and great difference (as there must needs be betwixt Scripture and no Scripture) yet to those that are unable to discern so much, the matter stands overruled only by the authority of the Church. For though, as Master Hooker saith, the "Scriptures teach us that saving truth which God hath discovered to the world by revelation; yet it presumeth us taught otherwise, That itself is divine and sacred:" and therefore, the reading of the Scripture in our Churches, is one of the plainest evidences we have of the Church's assent and acknowledgment that it is the Scripture: and yet, without any contradiction at all, whoso assenteth to the words of eternal life, doth it in regard of his authority whose words they are. Those with whom the Church is to deal are, often, heretics; and these will much sooner believe the Church, than the Scriptures. Therefore saith St. Austin, (in that known place) "I had not believed the Scriptures, if I had not been compelled by the authority of the Church."* And howsoever the Church may seem now little to need her authority, because the greatest harvest of heresies is past; yet we must not contemn her for all that, because even the weeds of heresy being grown unto a ripeness, do even in their very cutting down scatter,

---

.　　　　†Dr. Whitaker.　　　* Contra epist. fundamenti. cap. 5

oftentimes, those seeds which for awhile lie unseen and buried in the earth, but afterwards freshly spring up again, no less pernicious than at the first. Therefore the Church hath, and must have, to the end of the world, four singular offices towards the Scripture.† First, to be a *witness* and keeper of them, as it were a faithful register: whose fidelity, in that behalf, unless we be bastard children, we have no reason at all to suspect; witnesses of less truth and authority, having oftentimes the credit to be believed. Secondly, to discern and *judge* between false and adulterate, and that which is true, and perfect; in this respect, it hath a property which other assemblies want; to hear, and discern the voice of her Husband; neither can she be thought a chaste spouse, who hath not the ability to do that. But as the goldsmith either in his balance, or with his touchstone, discerneth pure gold from other metals of less value, yet doth not make it; so dealeth the Church, who hath not authority to make Scripture, that which is not; but maketh a true difference from that which did only seem. Neither in this respect, is the Church above the Scriptures, but acknowledgeth in humility, that she is left in trust, to tell her children which is her husband's voice; and to point out to the world (as John Baptist did Christ) a truth of a far more excellent perfection than herself is: as, if I doubted of a strange coin, wherein I rest satisfied in the resolution of a skilful man; but yet valuing the coin for the matter and the stamp of the coin itself. The third office of the Church is to *publish*, and divulge; to proclaim as a crier, the true edict of our Lord himself; not daring (as Chrysostom saith) to add any thing of her own;‡ which she no sooner doth, but the true subjects yield obedience, not for the voice of him that proclaimeth, but for the authority of him whose ordinances are proclaimed. The last is to be an *Interpreter;* and in that following the safest rule (to make an undivided unity of the Truth incapable of contradiction) to be a most faithful expositor of his [*its*] own meaning. Thus whilst the Church for that trust reposed in her, dealeth faithfully in these points, we are not

---

† Testis, Vindex, Præco, Interpres.   ‡ Homil. il ad Titum.

24

afraid to acknowledge, that we so esteem of the Scriptures, as rightly we are led by the authority of God's Church. Those that are of that judgment, that they dare give credit without witness, though we follow not in their example in overmuch credulity, yet we blame not their judgments in that kind. Touching therefore the Authority of the Church and the Scriptures, though we grant (as you say), that the Church is truly distinguished by the Scriptures; that the Scriptures (which is a strange phrase) "warrant the trial of God's word;" and that it was ever believed for the Word's sake; yet without fear of "underpropping" any "popish principle" (as you term it) we say, that we are taught to receive it, from the authority of the Church; we see her judgment; we hear her voice; and in humility subscribe unto all this; ever acknowledging the Scriptures to direct the Church, and yet the Church to afford (as she is bound) her true testimony to the Scripture. For the verse of Menander, Aratus,† or Epimenides,‡ was, and had been ever but the saying of poets; had not the Church assured us, that it was uttered since, by an instrument of the Holy Ghost.

---

†Acts xvii. 28.   ‡Tit. i. 12.

ARTICLE V.

OF FREEWILL

In searching out the nature of Human reason, whilst we reach into the depth of that excellency which man had by creation; we must needs confess, that by sin he hath lost much who now is unable to comprehend all that he should; but we dare not affirm that he hath lost all, who, even in this blindness, is able to see something; and, in this weakness, strong enough, without the light of supernatural justifying grace, to tread out those paths of moral virtues which have not only great use in human society, but are also not altogether of a nature oppositely different from man's salvation. And therefore, the natural way to find out Laws by Reason, guideth, as it were by a direct path, the Will unto that which is good, which naturally having a freedom in herself, "is apt to take, or refuse, any particular object whatsoever being presented unto it."§ Which though we affirm, yet we neither say that Reason can guide the Will unto all that is good (for though every good that concerneth us hath evidence enough for itself, yet reason is not diligent to search it out); nor we say not, that the Will doth take or refuse any particular object; but is apt rather, noting the nature whereby it hath that power, than shewing the ability whereby it hath that strength. For though sin hath given (as the schoolmen observe) four wounds unto out nature; "Ignorance, Malice, Concupiscence, and Infirmity;" the first, in the understanding; the second, in the will; the third, in our desiring appetite; the last, in the irascible; yet the Will is free from necessity and coaction; though not from misery and infirmity. For (as St. Bernard saith) there is a threefold freedom; from necessity, from sin, from misery: the first, of nature; the second, of grace; the third, of glory.* In the first, from the bondage of coaction, the Will is free in it [*its*] own nature, and hath power over itself. In the second, the Will is not free, but freed from the bondage of sin. And in the third, it is freed from the servitude of corruption. Now that freedom, by which the Will of man is named free, is the first only: and therefore we dare say, that the wicked, who have not the two last (being captives to sin in this life, and to misery in the life to come), yet for all this, want not the freedom of Will. Now this freedom of nature, as Aristotle noteth, is two-fold; that which is opposite to a simple coaction, and that to which not only a coaction, but a necessity is opposite.† The first is of those things, which cannot by any means but be willed of us, and yet freely and voluntarily are willed; as to be happy, which none can choose but will, though most do fail in the means: the second, when we can either will, or not will; as to walk, speak, sit, or such like. Now because nothing is the proper, or the chief object of the Will, but that which either is, or seems to be, good, as all learned men affirm;‡ therefore in our Wills, there is this usual error, That our understandings are deceived by the inferior appetite of the flesh, which maketh that seem good, in the particular proposition, which it pronounceth to be evil, in the general.§ And therefore, being by nature to will good, willeth that which is directly opposite; because reason growing idle, in the sloth of an inferior appetite, wanteth diligence to search it out. Few men but think drunkenness in general to be evil; which notwithstanding themselves do embrace, because in particular they think it good. This being the difference in all sin, that then it seemeth to be none, when it is–this sin. Thus, the conclusion, by the rules of Logic, being from the particular (wherein

---

* "De gratia et libro arbitrio, &c." P. LOMB. Sent. lib. ii. dist. 25. 1 Cor. vii. 36. Libera sed liberata. Rom. vi. 7. *Ibid.* iii.

† Aristot. Ethic. lib. iii. cap. 4,5.

‡ Clem. Alexan. in Strom. Aug. Confess. lib. ii. cap. 6. Boeth. de Con. lib. iv. Damasc. de Fide, lib. ii. cap. 22. Arist. Eth. lib. i. cap. 1. Senec. de Ben. lib. iv. cap. 7.

§ "In hypothesi bonum, in thesi malum."

reason corrupted hath failed), the Will hath reason enough to follow that; and therefore saith St. Austin, "man using amiss the freedom of this Will, hath both lost it and himself;"§ not in respect of the natural liberty from coaction, but in respect of the liberty which is from sin, as Aquinas answereth.* St. Ambrose (or whosoever was the author of that book of The calling of the Gentiles) saith, That in man there is a threefold Will; Sensitive, Animal, Spiritual; the two first, he holdeth to be free; the last, to be the work of the Holy Ghost. For as one noteth, "There is in man an understanding of earthly things, and of heavenly:—*earthly* things, as of a policy, governing of families, arts, liberal and mechanical, and such like, which pertain not directly to God, to his kingdom, to the righteousness of it, to eternal happiness; *heavenly*, as the knowledge of the Divine Will, and framing our lives according to it. Of the first, we say, That because man is a sociable creature, and naturally inclineth to all that concern the preservation of that; there are left in him certain universal impressions, wherein, in all ages, wise men have conspired for the making of good laws."† Which in my opinion is not much less, than that which you reprehend, being affirmed by Mr. Hooker. But the understanding of heavenly things, we confess, by the corruption of original sin, wholly to be taken from us. For natural things are corrupted, and supernatural taken away.‡ For we think not as some of the ancient Fathers did, especially the Greeks (who were loath to dissent too much from the Philosophers), That man was corrupted only in his sensual part, and that he hath Reason sound, and his Will also for the most part. For saith St. Austin, "Adam had that he might if he would; but not to will that he could."‖ And therefore, in supernatural things (which are the works of piety, pleasing and acceptable to God), by grace:"‖ yet for all this, neither doth the Will want in his [*its*] own nature a

---

§ AUG.. in Ench. cap. 30.   * Part. I. quest. 83. art. 2.
† Calv. Inst. lib. ii. cap. 2. sect. 13. "Inspersum est universis semen aliquod ordinis politici." [*Ib. in fin.*]
‡ "Naturalia corrupta; supernaturalia ablata."   ‖ De Corrept. et gratia, ad Valent. cap. 2
‖ "Humana voluntas non libertate gratiam, sed gratia consequitur libertatem." AUG. *ubi supra.*

potential freedom in all things, nor an actual powerful freedom in some things;§ for the blow that sin gave, made not an equal disability to all actions; seeing all actions are not in equal distance from man's nature. For the thoughts and the actions of man, we know are of three kinds; natural, moral, supernatural; now there are many truths theorical, and mechanical, contained in natural and human arts, which by man may be comprehended, only by the light of nature: for though some divines are of opinion that no moral truth can be known of the understanding of man, in the state of nature corrupt, without the special help of God;* others contrary (as Albertus, Bonaventure, Scotus, Aquinas and divers others) yet all agree in this, That a man can know a moral truth in general, without any special grace; but that good that directly belongeth to eternal life he cannot. Now what, I pray you, doth our Church say less when it saith, That "without the grace of God (which is by Christ) preventing us, that we will, and working together while we will; we are nothing at all able to do the works of piety which are pleasing and acceptable to God?" Or, what in your opinion doth Mr. Hooker say more, when he saith That "there is in the will of man naturally that freedom, whereby it is apt" (not able) "to take or refuse any particular object whatsoever, being presented to it?" or when he saith, "there is not that good which concerneth us, but it hath enough for evidence in itself if Reason were diligent to search it out:" the fault of man's error in election, arising out of the sloth of reason, not out of the nature of the good. And this sloth being nothing else but that heavy burthen wherewith we are laden by our first corruption. And therefore, in mine opinion, the accusation is directly false, whereby you would make him to say contrary to his words: that "Reason by diligence is able to find out any good concerning us." For he that saith that there is virtue enough in the pool to heal, if a man had power enough to put himself in; doth not affirm that man hath strength

---

§ "Cum vult non potest, quia quando potuit noluit: ideo per malum velle perdidit bonum posse." AUG.

* Calv. Instit. lib. i. cap. 2. et lib. ii. cap. 2. Grego. Arimi. in Sent. 2. dist. 26. quest. 1. art. 1. Gaspar. Cassalius, de Quadripartita justitia, lib. i. cap. 32.

enough to do it; but that the pool had virtue, if he were able to do it.† But doubtless "we are dead in our sins, and trespasses;"‡ "we are not sufficient of ourselves to think any thing;"§ and yet, as Seneca saith, It is the gift of God that we live, for that he hath done without us; but it is an act of our own (not simply, but of ourselves helped) that we live well."‖ "For many other things may unwillingly be done by us, but the act of believing, as it must be done in us, so it must be done willingly, and with us. and, therefore, saith St. Austin, there are three things necessary that supernatural mysteries may be perceived by us; first, a divine revelation from the Scriptures; a persuasion of that truth by miracles, or some other means; and last of all, the rule of the Will.¶ For, saith he, "a man may enter into the Church unwillingly; he may receive the sacrament unwillingly; but no man can believe but willingly." Now there is no difference betwixt the will, and the freewill (both being the rational power of desiring), but that the one respecteth the end, and then it is called Will: the other respecteth the means, and then it is called Free-will. So the same power of understanding, as it respecteth the first principles, is called Understanding; as it respecteth the conclusion which is gathered by a discourse, from the principles, it is called Reason. Now this Reason concerning things doubtful, hath naturally in itself, a way to both opposites; but leaneth to that for the most part whereunto either appetite, ignorance, or grace sway it. So that though freely and without constraint, it follow naturally the wisdom of the flesh; yet without a supernatural grace, "the wisdom of the flesh is enmity against God: for it is not subject to the law of God, neither indeed can be.* This being duly weighed with understanding, and considered of with a charitable humility, such as the cause requireth, every man may see (notwithstanding your accusation) that our Church in this neither differeth from the truth, nor Master Hooker at all from our Church.

---

† John v. 7.　　　　‡ Ephes. ii. 5.　　　　§ 2 Cor. iii. 5.
‖ "Deorum munus est quod vivimus, nostrum quod sancte vivimus." SENEC.
¶ Rom. x. "Imperium voluntatis." AUG. *in Johan. tract.* 36.　　* Rom. viii. 7.

ARTICLE VI.

OF FAITH AND WORKS.

Where charity hath not power enough to guide reason, there malice, out of ignorance, is able to make conclusions against sense. For the eyes being blinded, which, naturally, are to perform the best offices of seeing; the colours that are discerned otherwise, are little better than the false errors of a troubled fancy. For "where the light is darkness, how great must that darkness be?"† To attain, by a supernatural power, to that felicity, which is an act of the greatest mercy, as infinite numbers fail in the thing; so there are not a few, which utterly mistake the means. And whilst all that are Christians, acknowledge it to be a grace; eager contentions are stirred up, Whether it be imputed, or inherent, in us? And seeing in this act of justification, by the consent of all, man doth receive from God what he hath, the question is, What virtue must be in that hand, to enable weakness to receive such strength: and, how that faith must be accompanied, that is able to clothe our souls with the righteousness of another's merit? Here we have adversaries, whom peradventure we mistake, as they mistake us; making (as in other points) a misconstruction, to be the ground of a great difference; and the strongest opposition, to arise from hence; that neither part is willing to understand each other. Here, if we

---

† Matt. vi. 23.

should but discover the least means of reconcilement, some hasty spirits would not stick to accuse us as more than partial; and that treacherously we sought to betray the cause. In that we purpose to set down what Truth warranteth in this behalf, it is rather to free him from suspicion whom you do accuse, than that he in that wherein you accuse him, any way standeth in need of our weak defence. If man rightly value but the merit of the Son of God; and, how so humble, and innocent obedience, to so low a state, must needs in justice, make a full satisfaction, for so great a sin; he cannot choose but confess that "Only for the merit of our Lord and Saviour Jesus Christ through faith, and not for works and our merits, we are accounted righteous before God."* If the soul of man, did serve only to give him being in *this* life, then things appertaining to this life would content him, as we see they do other creatures; which creatures, enjoying those things by which they live, they do seek no further, but in this contentation, do shew a kind of acknowledgment that there is no higher good which, any way, doth belong unto them. With man it is far otherwise; for although all inferior things were in the possession of one, yet he would ever with a desire thirst for something above all those; so that nature, even in this life, doth claim a perfection, higher and more divine than any thing in itself,† which man must receive in the reward: now rewards do always presuppose such duties performed as are rewardable;‡ our natural means unto blessedness are our Works, nor is it possible, that nature should ever find any other way to Salvation, but only this. Yet seeing that no man can say, since the foundation of the world, that his Works are pure, but that all flesh is guilty of that, for which God hath threatened eternally to punish; there resteth either no way unto salvation, or a way which must needs be supernatural, and above man's reach. Had Adam continued in his first estate, man's absolute righteousness and integrity in all his actions, had been the way of life to him and to all his posterity; though, peradventure, not in so large a manner as heavenly

---

* Art. 11. Eccles. Angl. de Hominis justificat.
† "Summa merces est ut ipso perfruamur." AUG *de Doct. Christi*, cap. 6.
‡ Matt. vii. 11.

felicity doth import; the possession whereof, even the least moment, were too abundant a retribution. Yet now, we failing in that which was our duty, it were a thing impossible in nature, to obtain the other. The light of nature is never able to find out any way of obtaining the reward of bliss, but by performing exactly the works of righteousness. Therefore God hath prepared a supernatural way, namely that we do "believe;"§ "not that God doth require nothing unto happiness, at the hands of men (as Master Hooker saith), saving only a naked Faith (for Hope and Charity we may not exclude) but that without Faith all other things are as nothing;" this "being the ground of those other divine virtues." "The principal object of Faith, is that eternal verity, which hath discovered the treasures, of hidden wisdom in Christ; the highest object of Hope, is that everlasting goodness, which in Christ doth quicken the dead; the final object of Charity, is that incomprehensible beauty, which shineth in the countenance of Christ, the Son of the living God. The first beginneth here, with a weak apprehension of things not seen, and endeth in the beholding of God in the world to come. The second beginneth here, with a trembling expectation of things far removed, and as yet, but only heard of; and endeth with a real and actual fruition, of that which no tongue is able to express. The third beginneth here, with a weak inclination of heart towards him, unto whom, we are not able to approach, and endeth with an endless union; the mystery whereof, is higher, than the reach of the thoughts of men." And howsoever the apprehension of that righteousness whereby man is justified, be properly but the work of one, yet we dare not (neither do any learned in our Church) make Faith to be naked of other virtues; and therefore it is so much the more strange, that you follow the error which our adversaries have accused us for, as though it were an opinion holden by our Church. In this article against Master Hooker, you say, that God requireth no more at the hands of men, unto happiness, than "a naked belief." And a little after; "We claim nothing, by any duty we do or can do, or any virtue which we find in ourselves, but only by that

---

§ John vi. 29.

naked faith," &c. In these assertions (which are repugnant to our Church), and, in the best construction, make but a harsh sound; what do you else, but discover that error which they of the Church of Rome, by a mistaking, have thought us to hold? as though it were our doctrine, that we could be justified, by a Faith that were merely "naked?" Luther striving to shew how little our Works did, in the merit of man's Salvation, speaketh somewhat harshly, when he saith, "Faith without and before we have charity, doth justify."† And in another place (both which are not unjustly called in question by those of the Church of Rome) he saith; "Faith unless it be without even the least good Works, doth not justify; nay, it is no faith.‡ But Master Calvin speaketh in this, better than either Luther or you; Faith alone justifieth, but not that faith which is alone.§ For if our Church held a "naked" Faith (which none that were wise ever did), might not all the world justly accuse us as enemies to good Works? The most learned in Germany held a necessity of good Works; "not a necessity of effecting, but a necessity of presence;"‖ for we are saved doubtless by grace, but (having years) we cannot ordinarily be saved unless we have good Works.** For Faith which we teach to justify, is not void of good Works; as Dr. Fulke answereth to the Rheims' objection.†† And therefore, in another place, he saith, "the elect are always fruitful of good Works."‡‡ From hence, (seeing faith hath no assurance for itself either to God or to man) we exhort in our sermons to good Works, we persuade to humiliation, by fasting and weeping; which are (if they be truly penitent) means to blot out sin, through God's unspeakable and undeserved mercy. For as St. Paul saith, "Godly sorrow causeth repentance unto salvation, not to be repented of:"§ And therefore, saith St. Jerome, "fasting and sackcloth are the armour of repentance." "And that men please God by fasting (saith Dr. Fulke) as Anna, Tobie, Judith, Hester,

---

†"Fides et sine et ante charitatem justificat." LUTH. *in* 2. *ad Gal.*

‡ LUTH. Tom. I. prop. 3. "Fides nisi sit sine ullis etiam minimis operibus non justificat, imo non est fides."

§ In Anti Concil. ad art. 11. sess. 6.

‖ Melancthon. Brent. Chemnis. Calvin. Inst. lib. iii. cap. 16. "Necessitas præsentiæ, non efficientiæ."

** "Gratia salvamur, sed non absque bonis operibus." CLEM. ALEXAND. *Strom.* 5.

††In Jac. ii. annot. 11.　　　　　　‡‡ In Matt. xxv. annot. 3

we doubt nothing at all while we use it to the right end allowed of God; that is, humbling of ourselves, and chastising of our bodies that it [*they*] might be more obedient to the Spirit, and fervent in prayer."‖ Nay, our solemn Fasts are, as Mr. Hooker saith, "the splendour, and outward glory of our religion; forcible witnesses of ancient truth; provocations to the exercise of all piety; shadows of our endless felicity in heaven; and everlasting records and memorials upon earth;"¶ which, it is great pity it is so much neglected, because even therein, they which cannot be drawn to hearken unto what we teach might only by looking upon that we do, in a manner read whatsoever we believe. Now, that he saith, the "attainment unto any gracious benefit of God's unspeakable and undeserved mercy, the phrase of antiquity hath called by the name of Merit;"** this is that, wherein you desire to be resolved. And surely, he hath read little, who is ignorant that the heathen Masters of the Latin tongue, and the Fathers for antiquity, nearest unto those times, have used the word (Merit) far in another sense, than that whereunto the violence of some constructions have wrested it at this day.†† And Aquinas himself understandeth by the name of Merit, not a Work not due, which should deserve a reward; but a Work which mercifully, and by the goodness of God, a reward followeth. The phrase of the Latin doth properly make one to *merit* of another, and, as it were, to bind him to him who doth any thing which pleaseth and delighteth him, for whom it is done. Thus that place in the Epistle to the Hebrews, "To do good, and to distribute, forget not; for with such sacrifice God is *well pleased.*" Where they of Rhemes, following the Latin, *promeretur*, say "promerited;" shewing that they meant nothing else in ancient time, by Merit, but that delight, allowance, and contentment, which God taketh in those good things we do, and so rewardeth them. And Dr. Fulke confesseth that

---

§ Cor. vii. 10. ‖ In Rhem. Test. Matt. xv. annot. 3
Meriting for obtaining: so in the Confession of Wittenburg.
¶Casaubon. in Pl. Epist. Mereri stipendia. Calv. Inst. lib. iii. cap. —sect. 2. Usi sunt (fateor) passim vetusti ecclesiæ scriptores, atque utinam voculæ unius (abusu) (so that it properly signifieth otherwise) erroris materiam posteris non præbuissent. Mark, the word (præbuissent) gave but only occasion.

Primasius, who was St. Austin's scholar, used the same word, *promeretur,*** as it was taken amongst the vulgar at that day, far differing from the sense wherein it is now used. Thus much briefly, may serve for answer in this point; That Faith is not alone, though alone it justify; that though a man sin, (if he repent) his Faith may save him; that there are uses (nayexcellent uses) of good Works, though they do not save us; and last of all, if posterity had not corrupted the word *merit*, that we would not be afraid to speak in the phrase of antiquity, and call our virtuous attainment (by mercy of grace) by the name of *merit.*‡

¶Heb. xiii. 16.   ** Pleased.

‡ ["It cannot be denied by any modesty, but that the words εὐαρεστεῖται ὁ θεὸς signify that 'God is well pleased,' or God is pleased; and, therefore, that our translation is true, and the Vulgate not so, or at the least not so due. And the Vulgate, and the Jesuits after it, having so translated it before (in chap. xi. 5, 6), it is so much the greater fault there (in chap. xiii.) not to give the same weight of words in the translation, where the same valuation is in the original. And although the ancient writers, as Primasius following this translation, and Cyprian as they have alleged him before (p. 18 of their Pref.), use this word (promeretur), yet that they vary from this Popish sense of Meriting, this one sentence of Jerom doth notable declare; so much the more to be regarded as the Jesuits will needs have this translation [the Vulgate] Jerom's. Let therefore Jerom himself, the father, as they say, of this translation, expound himself. 'It is,' saith he (in Epist. ad Rom. cap. iv.), ' a great blessedness to deserve the grace of God without the labour of the Law and of Repentance, as when one receiveth a dignity of nought;' that which, what can be more pregnant to the advancement of God's free Grace, without all manner of Work? Look also at Pontianus (in Vita Cyp.) which was Cyprian's Deacon, who useth the same word that Cyprian declareth that his meaning is no other than that God is *pleased* with such good duties." CARTWRIGHT'S *Confut. of the Rhemist Test.* p. 650.]

ARTICLE VII.

THE VIRTUE OF WORKS.

As goodness, so Truth being but one, whatsoever is opposite (be it never so carefully observed) in the course of a long stream, at the last foldeth itself in a contradiction. For falsehood hath no more strength to prove a truth; than truth hath weakness to beget a lie. Then, the ground of all true assertions concurring immovably in that one first truth, of which all other inferior are but branches; whatsoever goeth about to disprove that, must of necessity, in his [*its*] own parts be divers, and imply a contrariety, seeing it laboureth to infringe the certainty of that which, eternally and unchangeably, is but one. Hence cometh it, that unskillful men (the grounds of whose opinions are but the uncertainties of their own ignorance) are thought to want memory whilst they contradict themselves; when indeed, the defect is in judgment, which cannot make Truth the ground of their knowledge; from which, if they swerve never so little, they do not sooner oppugn others, than cross themselves; truth admitting no coherence of contrarieties, seeing itself is but only one. From this hath proceeded that oversight of a great number, who speaking first against a truth uttered by others; come at length to speak even directly against themselves. Thus you that in the former Article, disputed of Faith, "naked" and destitute of all good Works, make your next step to those good Works that do accompany Faith. Where I understand not (but perhaps you do) why you call them good, if they arise not naturally out of Faith; or, why you call that Faith "naked" which is accompanied with these good Works. But, doubtless, there being a moral goodness, even where there is want of supernatural light; and the most certain token of that goodness being—if the general persuasion of all men do so account it; it cannot choose, but seem strange, that the approbation of these, should, in your opinion, be applied to those works that are done out of faith, after man is justified; seeing there is a good (as Mr. Hooker saith) that doth follow unto all things by observing the course of their nature; yet natural agents cannot obtain either reward, or punishment: for amongst creatures in this world, only man's observation of the law of his nature (because he hath will) is righteousness; only man's transgression sin. For even to do that, which nature telleth us we ought (howsoever we know it) must needs be acceptable in God's sight. How this, uttered out of great judgment to another purpose (namely, that good things are done, and allowed, whereof we have other direction than Scripture) is by you wrested against the Articles of our Church, either concerning the perfection of Works which are with Faith, or the goodness of Works without Faith; to say plainly, I cannot yet understand! Therefore, as the dealing is unequal, to make him say what you list, so the advantage is too great, to make him an adversary to a cause of your own making; when the whole scope of his speech is to another purpose. For there is no indifferent reader but had he considered what Mr. Hooker speaketh, and to what end, in those places by you alleged; he must of necessity have wondered at your sharp and acute judgments, what would, without blushing, adventure to allege him to that end. But an opinion, doubtless, that these things would never be examined, gave that confidence to your first motion; which consideration would have hindered, if you had but once dreamed to have been called in question. We should not, therefore, need in this, much to defend him; but, briefly resolve you, what our Church holdeth (and fitly) in this point. The "Articles of our Church which ye think are oppugned, are two; first, that "the fruits of Faith, cannot abide the severity of God's justice;" that man out of Faith, doth good Works, which, though they make us not just, yet are both acceptable, and rewardable: I doubt not but it is a truth, whereof if ye had not been persuaded, this Letter of yours (profitable, as you think, to the Church, and pleasing to God), as all the rest of your writings in that kind, had lain buried, unborn, in those rotten sepulchres from whence into the world they did first come; whilst we are by that intermediate justice of Christ, made righteous, and have obtained a free remission of our sins, that we are termed just; there is with this mercy joined the Holy Ghost; which dwelling in us, maketh us fruitful to good Works; this reviving all parts from our natural corruption, reformeth us to a pure and willing obedience unto that revealed Will, which is the rule of all that we ought to do: yet, seeing we are clothed with corruption, there are, even in our best actions, those remainders of imperfection which serve to teach us thankfulness and humility, both arising from the consideration of our own weakness. And I doubt not, but even in this point, many of the Church of Rome (whose humiliation in their penitency of heart, seemeth far to exceed ours) are of this opinion, That even the best action performed in their whole life (as there are yet some few monuments spared from the covetous hand) if all points of it were considered with a straight view, sifting even the least circumstances which closely insinuate themselves out of our corruptions into our actions; they would (I say) confess, that there is something which tasteth of the flesh: which corruption, if either for want of a strict consideration we see not, or through a self-love could pardon, yet it is not able, in the feebleness of his [*its*] own nature, to abide the exact trial and severity of God's judgment. That law, the least transgression whereof is sin, is said to be fulfilled three ways; first "in Christ;"† and so all the faithful are said to fulfil the law, having his obedience imputed to them. Secondly, it is fulfilled by a divine acceptation; for God accepteth our obedience begun, as if it were perfect; seeing what imperfections are in it, are not imputed to us. For it is all one, not to be, and not to be imputed; "blessedness"‡ being the reward of both: and we know that there is no condemnation to those that are in Christ Jesus."§ Thirdly, it is fulfilled by us: an error I think scarce any do hold, saving only the Anabaptists. For that eternal Wisdom, which hath led man by the Law unto Christ,

---

† Rom. viii. 1. 1 Cor. i. 30.   ‡ Psal. xxxii. 1.
§ Rom. viii. 1.

hath set those bounds, which all men have broken, (the first commandment and the last*) to include all, as guilty of the breach of the whole law: For "our knowledge being but in part, it is not possible (saith St. Austin) that our love can be perfect."†
And therefore, we conclude the first point, according to the Article of our Church, from which there is no syllable in Master Hooker that is different; That our Works, though they be good, and so esteemed and rewarded, yet they cannot abide the justice of the law, and the severity of God's judgment. The second point is, Whether the Works which are done before the grace of Christ, are not only not acceptable to God, but also have the nature of sin. In this we must use some care; for whilst men, justly disagreeing, have equally laboured to be different one from another; both in the end, have been equally distant from the truth. That there are excellent graces in the heathen, no man doubteth; and he must needs be far from reason and sense, who maketh no difference betwixt the justice, moderation, and equity of Titus and Trajan, and the fury, violence, and tyranny of Caligula, Nero, and Domitian; betwixt the unclean lusts of Tiberius, and the continency, in this respect, of Vespasian; in one word, betwixt the observation, and the breach of Laws. For there is that difference betwixt just and unjust, that even the frame of nature (where sense wanteth) acknowledge a well being, by the observation of what it ought: and therefore, much more in those good Works, which because they missed of the right scope, we dare not call by the name of true, perfect, Christian virtues; yet for their very action, we are content (so long as they swerve not from the righteousness of the law of nature) to give them leave to be called by a better name, than only sins; and yet for all this, no man taketh them to be much better in the true severity of a hard construction; for those that are not regenerate, although they sin in their best observation of the moral law, yet is much better to perform those offices than to perform them not; seeing "a part of that endeavour, though it be not mere righteousness, yet it is less sin."‡ We

---

* 1. Diliges Dominum Deum tuum, &c. 2. Non concupisces, &c.

†Aug. Tom. III. de Sp. et lit. cap. ult.

‡Zanch. de Relig. lib. i. cap. 6.

must, therefore, remember, that a Work is considerable, either in respect of the substance; or in regard of the manner of doing. In respect of the Work, all the actions of infidels are not sin; seeing they perform those things which are commanded, by the law of nature, of nations, of God; nay they are so far, in this respect, from being sins, that (as St. Austin saith) God doth plenteously reward them. But concerning the manner of working, all their actions are sin; as proceeding from a corrupt fountain; a heart that wanteth true Faith; and directed to an end of less value than He is, whose glory ought to be the end of all we do. This is confessed even by our adversaries themselves, with whom seeing we do agree, there can be no suspicion that we should dissent from that which our Church holdeth; and this may serve rather to tell you what, in these points, is the judgment of our Church, than to defend him whose words you have wrested, to a far different sense.

ARTICLE VIII.

WORKS OF SUPEREROGATION.

The nearness, oftentimes to evil, is warrant enough for suspicion, to accuse of evil; and because all errors are not equally distant from truth, some men, in their true assertions, are supposed, by weak judgments, not to differ at all from error. From hence cometh it, that those men (who have no other judgment but zeal; which is the best excuse I can make for your accusation in this article) have run so far, with a desire of safety, from those opinions that were thought dangerous, that they have come at length unto those that were much more dangerous, in truth. Which practice, though it argue a good care, yet it proceedeth from a timorous nature, wanting the ability to put a difference in the causes of true fear; so that this circumspection is but cowardliness; as he that were loath to be taken amongst his enemies' trenches, would get himself so far distant that he would outrun even the utmost limits of his own army. Thus have you dealt in this article; fearing to approve any thing that might tend to Supererogation, you have misliked even the allowance of those Works, which are good, and yet not commanded; for (say you) to hold, as Master Hooker doth, that God approveth more than he commandeth, what is it else, but to scatter even the grains of Popery, and to lead men, to those arrogant Works of Supererogation. Herein your fear, if it would have given you leave to have looked behind you, it may be peradventure, you would not have run away in such haste; especially in cases of no great danger. And therefore give me leave to tell you, that there is no treachery,

44

no danger, no cause of flying, from this opinion. All the unforced actions of men, are voluntary; and all voluntary actions, tending to their end, have choice; and all choice presupposeth the knowledge of some cause, wherefore we make it; and, therefore, "It is no absurdity to think that all actions of men, indued with the use of reason are generally either good, or evil. And although whatsoever is good, the same is also approved of God, yet according to the sundry degrees of goodness, the kinds of divine approbation are in like sort multiplied: for some things are good, yet in so mean a degree of goodness, that men are only not disproved, nor disallowed of God, for them: as that 'no man hateth his own flesh;' * it is a matter of approbation, and allowance, but of no great, or singular acceptation. So saith our Saviour, ' if you do good unto them that do so to you; the very Publicans themselves do as much:'"† Wherein to come short of them, as it were a great vice, so not to exceed them is no great virtue. "Some things in such sort are allowable, that they be also required as necessary to Salvation, by way of direct, immediate, and proper necessity final; so that without performance of such we cannot by ordinary course be saved; nor yet by any means be excluded from life, if we observe those." As nature gave light unto the former, so the Scripture is a guide to teach these; wherein, because all fail, it is the obedience and merit only of one, that must make all righteous, that must be saved. "Some things there are, although not so required of necessity, that to leave them undone excludeth from Salvation; yet not withstanding, are of so great dignity and acceptation with God, that most ample reward in heaven is laid up for them. Of these we have no commandment in nature, or Scripture, that doth exact them, in particular, at our hands; yet those motives there are, in both, which may serve to draw our minds most effectually to the performance of them. In this kind there is not the least action but it doth somewhat make to the accessory augmentation of our bliss;" which men have as much reason to desire, as to desire that they may be blessed; no

---

* Ephes. v. 29.   † Matt. v. 46.

measure of blessedness having power to content, saving only where the blessed wanteth capacity to receive greater. "Upon this dependeth, whatsoever difference there is between the states of saints in glory. Hereunto we refer whatsoever belongeth unto the highest perfection (for all perfection in this life is not equal) of man, by way of service toward God: hereunto that fervour and first love of Christians did bend itself, causing them to sell their possessions, and lay down the price at the blessed Apostles' feet; ‖ hereunto St. Paul, undoubtedly did aim, in so far abridging his own liberty, and exceeding that which the bond of necessary and enjoined duty tied him unto, to ease those Churches, to whom he preached," with his handy labour:** knowing that although it were not a duty which he was commanded, yet it was an advantage to his preaching, and acceptable to God; who doubtless approveth much more than he doth command. Thus when a man may live in the state of matrimony, seeking that good thereby which nature principally desireth; to make rather choice of a contrary life, in regard of St. Paul's judgment; he doth that which is manifestly allowed, and yet not commanded in God's Word;* because without any breach he might do otherwise. Thus when a man–who might lawfully possess his riches, yet willingly doth bestow them to religious uses, virtuously embracing that poverty which he esteemeth as an advantage to eternal riches–doth that which argueth a greater perfection, and for which he hath warrant, though no precept at all; because that which is a great virtue in him, is not a fault simply in those that do not the like. Precepts and counsels having this difference, that the one is of absolute necessity, the other left unto our free election, where both tending to the same end, yet in this differ, That both tend not after the same manner: both looking at the means, but the one after a more exquisite, and excelling perfection. For everyman being placed in this life betwixt the things of this world and spiritual good things, the more he cleaveth to these, the more perfect and excellent he is; and yet to cast them away wholly, is no precept of necessity, but an advice of greater perfection. He that

---

‖ Acts iv. 31.   ** 1 Thess. ii. 9.   * 1 Cor. vii. 6.

obeyeth not a precept, is guilty of deserved punishment; but he that faileth of these counsels, only wanteth, without sin, that measure of perfection. "For it is not a fault not to vow, but to vow and to perform, it is a praise."† He that performeth the one, shall have greater glory, but he that faileth in the other (without repentance) shall have certain punishment. Neither is it said, saith St. Austin, as thou shalt not commit adultery, thou shalt not kill; so thou shalt not marry, for "those are exacted, this is offered: this if it be done, it is praised; those unless they be done, they are punished."‡ For saith St. Jerome, where it is but advice, there is left a freedom; but where there is a precept, there is a necessity.§ Precepts are common to all; counsels the perfection of some few. The precept being observed, hath a reward; being not observed, a punishment: but a counsel, or advice, not observed, hath no punishment; and being observed, hath a greater reward. In these points all have not holden the same opinions; some thought these counsels to be of the same necessity with precepts; as those heretics called "Apostolici," mentioned by St. Austin‖ and Epiphanius.¶ Others esteemed them as things indifferent, and of no greater perfection.** Others as things forbidden;†† which error is accused by some of our adversaries, to be an opinion of our Church. He that, amongst us of learning, is most earnest in this point, is Peter Martyr; and all that any of them say, is but this; That these counsels are sin, if we esteem them as meritorious of themselves; That they are not sinful, but sometimes foolish; these men rather looking at the follies, which hath accompanied the superstition of some few, than the virtuous perfection, which attendeth upon the thing itself. Nay, there is none of any sound judgment in our Church, which doth not think, that willing poverty, humble obedience, and true chastity, are things very commendable, and do bring with them great advantage, to the true perfection of a Christian life; not that we can supermerit, by these, more than

---

† "Non est criminis non vovisse, sed vovisse et reddisse est laudis." AUG. *de Virg.* cap. 14.
‡ "Illa exiguntur, ista offeruntur, si fiant ista laudantur, nisi fiant illa damnantur." AUG.
§ Hieron. ad. Eustath.   ‖ Her. 40.   ¶ Her. 61.   **Joviniani; Vigilantii.
†† Aug. Her. 82.

we ought;* but that by these, we do more, than without these we should: for nature, commonwealths, and religion, as they have a being, so they refuse not a perfection, and a being well.

---

* "Proficientem coronabo, non proficientem non punio." CHRYSOST.

ARTICLE IX.

NONE FREE FROM ALL SIN.

It cannot choose but seem strange, that this should be an act of many, which, in the most favourable construction, cometh far short of that wisdom which should be in one. But it may be peradventure (that as it falleth out in things natural) actions are then best done, when one doth but one; distraction being a let to a finite power, and usually arising from diversity of judgments. For all not looking with the same eyes, nor following the like principles of understanding, though they agree in the general to reprehend, yet, for the most part, they fail in a particular resolution of what they think worthy to be reprehended. And therefore, as in elections, whilst two of the worthiest are competitors, stiff factions unite themselves in allowance of a third inferior to both. It seemeth that you have dealt so in this article, wherein either all your consents made a hinderance to what you meant; or, a division made you agree to mislike a thing of the least importance. Wherein if you had not discovered a weakness to be pitied, you might justly have expected an answer of more learning; but as men failing, even in those things wherein it is no great virtue not to fail, add little unto any man that shall direct them (because it is small praise to teach that which is a shame not to know), so to omit our direction, even where we wonder that any man should need it, must needs be esteemed, in a high degree, an unexcusable neglect of a necessary duty. No man I think (not of those that are thought to be out of the compass of the Church) maketh a doubt whether all men sin; leaving the

50

redemption of man, and so the freedom from sin, to him only who was eternally the Son of God. It was as necessary that he should be without sin, as it is certain that (except him) in many things we offend all. This is our frailty, That all of us do amiss, which we know; and the best of us do offend, when we know not; and therefore David with an humble heart, desired to be cleansed, from his "secret faults;" making that even a step, to keep him from "presumptuous sins."* As it is, therefore, an infirmity, that we do amiss in many things; so it is a virtue, that we would do amiss in nothing; this being the perfection of our country, and that the desire of our way: which, because (clothed with corruption) we cannot attain, we say daily (as we are taught) "Forgive us our trespasses." And they pray in vain to have sin pardoned, which seek not also by prayer to have sin prevented; yea every particular sin, except men can have some transgression wherewith they ought to have truce. "For although (saith Master Hooker) we cannot be free from all sin collectively" (that is in general, for so none was free saving only Christ) "in such sort that no part thereof shall be found inherent in us, yet distributively, at the least, all great and grievous actual offences, as they offer themselves one by one, both may, and ought by all means to be avoided; so that in this sense, to be preserved from all sin, is not impossible." This assertion seemeth in your opinions to be untrue; and for proof, you allege, "that we which are baptized, and regenerated, in many things do offend all; " did ever Master Hooker deny this? Nay in the very same place, are not these his words, "In many things we do all amiss?" But say you, if that be so, how can we avoid all great and grievous sins? Or, if we can, why may we not be preserved also, from all "small" sins; and so being free from both small and great, "preserve our robe pure, to the coming of our Saviour Christ?" In these few words, in my opinion, are three of the most strange and most violent conclusions that I have ever read; and those which are by no means agreeable to any Church. First, we say, "In *many* things we offend all;" therefore say you, In *all* things we offend all. Secondly, we say, we may

---

* Psalm xix. 12, 13.

"avoid some particular great and grievous sins;" therefore say you, why not *less* also? as if it were all one, not to sin all, and not to sin at all. Thirdly, we say, that we are to pray, and hope to be preserved from any and "every special sin;" therefore, say you, "we may keep our robe pure, to the coming of Christ." I would be loath to make evil arguments worse by repeating; and therefore I have used a direct sincerity in rehearsing your own words; wherein I shall not need to bestow any labour to overthrow a ruinous building of such weakness; but only to tell you, in these points, what is the judgment and sentence of the whole Church. First, no man doubteth but that all men are sinners; for "all the imaginations of the thoughts of man's heart are only evil continually."‡ In "iniquity are we born, and in sin are we conceived;"§ "who can understand his faults?"∥ For "the heart is deceitful, and wicked above all things, who can know it?"* For "unless a man be born of water and of the Spirit, he cannot enter into the kingdom of heaven."†† And "we are all by nature, the children of wrath."‡‡ In one word, none are free from sin, but he whom the blessed Virgin conceived, without the law of the flesh rebelling against the law of the mind; as St. Austin proveth most learnedly, by a cloud of witnesses of the ancient Fathers against Julian the Pelagian.§ Nay, even they of the Church of Rome, shew by their exorcising before baptism, that they think none to be without sin; where we do not now dispute of the lawfulness of that use, but by that conclude that, in this point, they hold a truth. So that the main thing which you so seem to mislike, is a thing not holden or defended (saving in some particular case, as the Virgin Mary) by any that I know; for even that stream of original sin, hath overflowed all mankind, out of which daily proceed those great and innumerable multitudes of actual sins. Your three false conclusions seem to establish a threefold error, contrary to the doctrine of all Churches that are accounted Christian. First, that all sin is but *one* sin. Secondly, that all sins are *equal*. Thirdly, that all sins are *united*. The first, making no division

‡ Gen. vi. 5.   § Psalm ii. 5.   ∥ Psalm xix. 12.   * Jer. xvii. 9.   † John iii. 5.
‡‡ Eph. ii. 3.   § Lib. i. et ii. Irenæus, Cyprian, Ræticius, Olympius, Hilarius, Ambros. Innocent, Greg. Naz. Basil, Chrysost. Hieron.

52

of the *kinds* of sin; the second, no distinction of the *qualities* of sin; and the third, no difference in *committing* sin. Against these, we say (and we hope warranted by truth), That sins are of divers kinds; of divers degrees; of divers natures; and that all are not, where one is. Sins then may be distinguished— in respect of the object against whom; God, our neighbour, ourself;—of the matter wherein; in the soul, ignorance, heresy; in the body, as the desires of the flesh;—from the manner of committing; of ignorance, infirmity, malice;—from the action itself; or our duty; of omission, of commission.‖— From the degrees, by which they rise; in the heart only; in the tongue, in the hands, or the work itself.— From the qualities of the persons; of Saints, which are venial, not imputed; of the wicked, mortal, for which they shall be condemned.— From the guilt; not pardonable, as the sin against the Holy Ghost; pardonable, not crying, or crying-sins;¶ as the shedding of innocent blood; the afflicting of the fatherless, or widow, the sin of Sodom; and last of all, the denying the labourers' wages: these are called crying-sins because, for their greatness, they call aloud for a great punishment. Others make a distinction of the seven Capital, or deadly-sins; which as we have no great reason to admit, so we have as little reason to disallow; knowing that even those are the heads and fountains of all sins of the second table. The second assertion which we hold is, That all sins are *not equal*; this was an opinion of the Stoics, who desirous to seem unwilling to commit the least, held an opinion that they were equal to the greatest; a good care, grounded upon an evil reason. If a pilot (say they) overturned a ship full of gold, he sinned no more than if he overturned a ship full of straw; for although there be a difference in the loss, yet the unskilfulness or negligence is all one. Or if two ere from the scope, even he that misseth a little, as well erreth, as he that misseth a great deal. But as in the former, of shipwreck, the fault was greater, because he had greater reason to make him circumspect; reason telling us that where we have mo [*more*] and stronger motives to do any thing, there we have less excuse, and the sin greater if we do not:

‖ Delicta a delinquendo, facinora a faciendo.
¶ Gen. iv. 10. Exod. xxii. 23, 27. Gen. xix. 13. Lam. v. 4.

for the latter, he erreth as well, but not as much; seeing both shooting at one mark, it is not all one, to be a foot and a rod wide. And therefore, that Law that forbad but one thing ("Thou shalt not kill") forbad three things, as Christ expoundeth it; anger to thy brother; to call him fool; to offer him violence; these having every one as their several degrees, so their several punishment. For who will say that the first is as great a fault as the second; or the third as small as the first; for doubtless, things, that are all forbidden, do in their own nature admit more or less. And howsoever, in some sort, virtues are called equal; yet vices are not: for all virtues, from the vanity of the world, tend but to one perfection (either to reason, as the Philosophers thought; or, to say better, to the revealed will of God, which is the rule of good and evil); but sins departing from this lead unto divers vanities, in divers kinds. Neither are virtues all equal simply, but by a kind of proportion; because they all proceed from the love of God, and all tend unto his glory: otherwise, in itself, faith is better than temperance, and one virtue may, in the same man, be far more excellent than in many others: as faith in the Centurion; obedience in Abraham; patience in Job. The consideration of this inequality of sin, as it acquainteth us with those steps that sin maketh in us; so it causeth us not to despair that we have committed some, but to hope and to be thankful, that we have escaped greater: "assuring ourselves (if we be not ourselves wanting) that though we cannot avoid all sins; yet we may and shall avoid all great and presumptuous sins. This heresy, then, we leave to his [*its*] first Authors,* Jovinian, and the rest; and so come to the last point: Because St. James saith, "he that keepeth the whole law, and offendeth in one, is guilty of all;"† some thought, all sins to be imputed unto him that committed any one; but St. James only telleth us, that God exacteth a keeping of them all. The Schoolmen, they interpet this place thus—In all sin, are two things; a departure from God, and a coming to the creature; which made St. Austin call sin, "an using of that which we ought to enjoy, and an enjoying of that, which we oughtbut to use,"* So that in respect of the departure, it

---

* Aug. Her. 82.   † James ii. 10.   * "Peccatum est utendis frui, et fruendis uti."

is true that St. James saith, he departeth as well from God, that committeth but one sin, as he that committeth many, but not so far. Therefore, to impose this upon us, were to add, even to those that are oppressed already, a burthen far greater, than the Law doth; for by obedience of the divine law, we tend from many to one; but by disobedience, from one to many; and those divers: and therefore, though virtues have, amongst themselves, their union and consent; yet vices have their dissent, nay their opposition. So that this, then, is the conclusion; That though no man be without all sin, yet many are without many presumptuous sins: which because through prayers and good means they avoid; it followeth not, an utter exclusion of all sin; nor, because they commit the least, it followeth not, that they offend equally, as if they committed all.

ARTICLE X.

OF PREDESTINATION.

Lest you should be like those whose humility ye are loath to imitate, ye have drawn your readers, in this Article, to a serious consideration of a deep point; letting them understand that ye are able, not only to advise sobriety to such rash presumers (as in your opinions Mr. Hooker is), but also to direct them in those points wherein, in your judgments, they are much deceived. That there is no man, how excellent soever, but without humility may easily err; I can as willingly confess it, as I commend such whom I see careful to give advice unto those that have gone astray. The one being the punishment of pride, to teach sobriety; the other the power of their learning, to shew humility; but that either he hath done the one, or you the other, in this Article, it is more than (as yet) I see any just inducements to believe. And I am sorry, that things of principal excellency should be thus bitten at, by men whom, it is like, God hath endued with graces, both of wit and learning, to better uses. For if all men had that indifferency of mind, that the greatest part of their forces were employed for the enlarging of that kingdom whereof all of us desire to be subjects; we should easily discern that a curious searching into that Will which is not revealed, serveth but to breed a contempt of that which is revealed unto us. Man desireth rather to know than to do; nay to know even those things which do not concern him, rather than to do that for the neglect whereof he must give an account. From hence cometh it to pass, that what the Schools have curiously sought out concerning the

56

nature of God's Will; the Pulpits, nay the Stalls of Artificers, have undertaken to decide them all. So that those things which once were but the deep amazement of some few, are now become the usual doctrine, and the vulgar consideration of many: where, that is not so much to be lamented which we search, and cannot comprehend; as that which we might comprehend but do not search: following, even that first evil exchange, for eating of the tree of the knowledge of good and evil, to deprive ourselves of the tasting of the tree of life.* So, that which nature once made a disease, the continuance of that disease hath made it nature; for even that light, which man whilst he wanteth liveth in perpetual darkness, is a light by our weakness not possible to be attained unto;† and those paths, which in our blindness we grope after with so much desire, they are "ways" not possible, by man's weakness, to be found out.‡ For there is "a cloud and darkness which are round about him,"§ and thick mists to cover him; for we are without proportion inferior to that power that hath first made us; not equal, not like. This being the just recompense of him that searcheth out that Majesty, in the end to be overwhelmed with the same glory.‖ Our greatest knowledge in this, saith St. Cyprian, is to confess our ignorance; for those acts that are of this nature, there is greater holiness to believe them, than to know them. "Truth lieth in the bottom, " as Democritus speaketh; and as Pindarus saith, "about our minds there hang innumerable errors;" therefore, the counsel of the son of Sirach is to be followed; "Seek not out the things that are too hard for thee, neither search the things rashly, which are too mighty for thee; but what God hath commanded thee, think upon that with reverence, and be not curious in many of his works; for it is not needful for thee to see with thine eyes, the things that are secret: be not curious in superfluous things, for many things are shewed unto thee above the capacity of men; the meddling with such, hath beguiled many, and an evil opinion hath deceived their judgment; thou canst not see without eyes." ¶ Yet for all this, to be absolutely either

---

* "Arbor Scientiæ complures privat arbore vitæ." Bonavent.
† "Lux inaccessibilis." 1 Tim. vi. 16.   ‡ "Investigabiles viæ ejus." Rom. xi. 33.
    § Psal. xcvii. 2.   ‖ Prov. xxv. 2.   ¶ Eccles. iii. 21–25.

ignorant or careless of those things that concern us, are no warrants for humility; but evidences of our sloth. The world at this day hath two sorts of men; whom, though we need not to respect much, yet, we are willing even to give them a reason of what we do; which, though peradventure they challenge at our hands, yet we demand not of them a reason of what they surmise. The first sort, are sensual and careless; neither respecting the will of God, of us, nor towards us: these, for the most part, understand nothing but earthly things; whom, if you remove to matters of a higher reach, you only arm them against yourself, and awake them to shew an insufferable contempt of all virtue. For that which they think painful to themselves, being idolaters to the belly, that they suppose partly impossible to others; and that which, for their own dulness, they cannot easily learn, that they imagine (but falsely) that others can as hardly teach. The second sort, wiser than these, think that we ought to search what God will have us to do; but, what he will do with us, or, what he hath decreed or determined of us, that they think ought wholly to be neglected by us. In these two errors, there is this difference; that the dangers being equal, the reasons are not equal, that do move both; seeing man hath mo [*more*] reasons to persuade him to know too little, than to know too much. Therefore the Church of England calleth Predestination unto life, "the eternal purpose of God, whereby, before the foundations of the world were laid, he constantly decreed by his counsel, unto us unknown, to deliver from the curse and destruction them whom he chose in Christ out of mankind; and as vessels made unto honour, through Christ to bring them to eternal salvation: whereupon, they who are endowed with so excellent a benefit of God, are called according to his purpose, and that by his Spirit, working in a fit time."* Wherein, if any thing in his general Will be opposite to that which secretly he hath determined of us, it is neither a contrariety in that essence which is but one; neither any warrant for us to be defective in our charity, which must imitate his general inclination to save all. And howsoever he grant not those prayers which we

---

*Art. XVII.

58

make for those who are not predestinate, because there is a more secret Will that "hath determined the contrary;" yet notwithstanding, even these prayers conformable to his general inclination, are in themselves without sin; they are our duties; and acceptable to God. For in God there is a Will revealed, which not to do is sin; and not revealed, which we may do and yet sin. And therefore, it must needs seem strange, that it is made a question by any, "How God eternally predestinateth by a constant decree, them whom he calleth and saveth, and yet hath a general inclination to save all? A matter easily answered, if we do but remember a two-fold Will: it is not, then, a foresight of any thing, that occasioned his Will otherwise; it is not any general election, altered upon a special cause; it is nothing either in us, or in himself, that maketh this decree, either to be at all, or to be any other, saving only one. We must know therefore, that the Will of God is secret; which therefore, in Scripture, is compared to a "deep,"* or revealed; which must be the rule of those actions which we ought to do. We may endeavour to do against the first and not sin, as Abraham in offering Isaac; I say endeavour, for no man can do against it: as also, fulfil the other, and yet sin, as Judas. This division of the Will of God, made by others (though in other terms), serveth both to answer such doubts as usually arise out of this darkness; as also, fully to satisfy those slender objections which you have framed in this point. Damascene divideth the Will into antecedent and consequent;† Peter Lombard, into his good pleasure, and the sign of it;* others, into a Will absolute, or conditional; others, into Will of us, or by us, to be done; St. Austin, into a most omnipotent, and most powerful Will, and into a Will not so powerful, that it ever cometh to pass:§ all these divisions concurring in one and the self-same thing, to teach us, that there be parts some revealed, some secret, of that which in his [its] own nature can no more be divers or many, than it is possible for the essence of the Godhead to be more than one. But how is it then (say you) that God willeth all men to be saved? Is it "a constant decree," or only "an inclination?" That he thus willeth,

---

§ Psalm xxxvi. 6. ‖ Lib. ii. 46. * Lib. i. dist. 45. §In Ench. 102, 103.

there is no man doubteth; and although some, with the restraint of the word "all,"∥ understand it, of his eternal, unchangeable, secret decree; yet we affirm, that with a conditional Will (which ever implieth faith and obedience); with a Will of the sign, antecedent, uneffectual, revealed, he willeth "all men to be saved." Who therefore that they [*sic*] are not, it is not his decree, but their own fault. And although we say, as Master Hooker doth, That God willeth many things conditionally; yet if we speak properly, all things that God willeth, he willeth simply; and therefore all things that God willeth, must be: the condition being, not in respect of the Will, but the manifestation of it. For it is no more possible that there should be a Will in God conditional, than that his knowledge and his wisdom should not be eternal: and yet in respect of us, who must be ruled by his Law, it is conditional. God sometimes commandeth what he will not have done; not that he is contrary in his Will, but that his will as yet is not wholly revealed. The matter of Predestination was never fully handled before the time of Pelagius, whose heresies gave occasion to St. Austin and others to confirm us in this point; wherein though I confess I unwillingly labour at this time, yet I doubt not to affirm (which may serve instead of answer to content you) that the Predestination of God is eternal, not conditional; immutable, not for works foreseen, and that those, which God hath determined (though his Predestination do not take away second causes) certainly must come to pass.* Neither is that any variableness, as you overboldly seem to insinuate, that he *inclineth* one way, and *decreeth* another; for certainly, saith St. Ambrose, he willeth all men to be saved, if they will, themselves; for he that hath given a law to all, doubtless hath excluded none.† Neither is here any acceptation of persons, That he hath chosen some, and not others; for that is acceptation of persons, saith St. Austin, when things to equals, equally due, are not equally divided; but where those things are divided, that are not due, but only of mere liberality bestowed, there this

‡ 1 Tim. ii. 4.   † By his revealed will.
§Bell. de Grat. et Lib. Arb. lib. ii. cap. 11, 12. Tom. III. Aqui. par. i. quest. 23.

inequality is without injustice, or acceptation of persons: it being in the power of a creditor that hath two debtors, to exact his due of the one without injustice, and, merely of his bounty, to forgive the other. If you go further in this point, to lead me into that depth, that lamentably hath swallowed up many thousands, I say with St. Austin; Thou O man, dost thou expect an answer of me, and [*when*] I am a man also? therefore let us rather both hear him, who saith, O man, who art thou, that doth answer God? reason thou, I will marvel; dispute thou, I will believe; and say, "Oh how unsearchable are his ways, and his judgments past finding out!"‡

---

‡ Rom. xi. 33.

ARTICLE XI.

THE VISIBLE CHURCH, AND THE CHURCH OF ROME

In the vehement dissensions of factions that are opposite, there is not a labour usually that reapeth either less fruit, or less thanks, than a charitable persuasion to a reconcilement; which, peradventure, hath been the principal cause why both parties looking, with a jealous eye, at the indifferent persuasions of a third, have continued both enemies in themselves, and yet the third suspected as a friend to neither. This, whilst men have done in kingdoms, their conclusions of peace have faintly languished; all sides earnestly wishing the thing, but suspecting those who were agents to intreat a persuasion to it: this, in the Church, some men have done, both in former times and of late, with more charity than either learning or success; so that, in the end, both parties have taken offence at the mention of a reconcilement. That the Church is at variance in itself, and so hath continued a long time, I think there is no man doubteth; and surely we are all persuaded, that unity and peace, are not fitter for any society in the world, than for that which is called by the name of "Church:" how this might be effected, it hath been the care of very wise men; who though they have found little appearance of success, by reason of those bad offices which uncharitable minds have performed, yet they have not ceased to wish in the behalf of the Church, as David did for Jerusalem, Oh that it were as a City built at unity in itself.* Private contentions are then furthest from all hope of agreement, when both parties, equally standing upon terms of superiority, earnestly contend which is most excellent; and, that neither have committed fault. In what straits the Church is, and

---

* Psalm cxxii. 3.

hath been in all times, it may easily be gathered in that, as yet, men are not resolved to whom it belongs principally to procure her "peace."† Some are of opinion that Princes must and ought to provide for the good and welfare of the Commonwealth; but as for Religion, they may lawfully permit to every man what his fancy desireth; so that the peace of their realms be not thereby troubled. This, once was the error of the heathen, who, admitting all sects of Philosophers, accounted it their honour that they refused none.‡ Whereupon saith Pope Leo, "This City (speaking of Rome), ignorant of the author of her advancement, whilst she hath ruled almost over all nations, hath basely been a servant to the errors of them all, and seemed to herself to have entertained a great religion, because she hath not refused the falsehood of any."§ This made Themistius the Philosopher (as Socrates reporteth‖) to persuade Valens the Emperor, That the variety of Sects was a thing much pleasing to God, seeing by that means he was worshipped after divers manners. This, though Constantine the Great did at the first (whose fact we will not at this time examine), yet, afterward, he commanded all the temples of the Idols to be shut up, and the Christian religion to be only used; ¶ whose sons, Constantius and Constantinus, so far followed (as St. Austin saith) the example of their Father, that Constantine threatened banishment to all those who rested not in the determination of the Nicene Council.‖ The contrary was practised by the Emperors Jovinian, Valens, and Julian; who, giving a liberty to all heretics, sought nothing more, than the overthrow of the Unity of the Church. But wise men have ever seen, that the peace and tranquility of the Commonwealth seldom or never ariseth but out of the concord and agreement of the Church itself.¶ The dissensions whereof, as they serve to hinder Religion, so they kindle that flame wherewithal, doubtless in the end, the Commonwealth itself must needs perish. But, how far all sides are from allowance of reconcilement, both the times present can testify too well, and the ages to come must needs witness, which shall possess a Church, as sons do the inheritance of contentious parents, the best part

---

† Ver. 6.   ‡ Aug. de Civitat. Dei. lib. xvii. cap. 51.   § Ser. 1. de SS. Petro et Paulo.
‖ Hist. lib. iv. cap. 27.   ¶ Euseb. lib. x. cap. 5.

whereof is wasted in unnecessary suits. The sound knowledge of Religion as well perishing in the midst of dissension, as the true practice doth fail by the plentiful abundance of too much peace. "There have been in the world, from the very first foundation thereof, but three religions; Paganism, which lived in the blindness of corrupt and depraved nature; Judaism, embracing the Law which reformed heathenish impiety, and taught salvation to be looked for through one whom God, in the last days, would send and exalt to be Lord of all; finally, Christianism, which yieldeth obedience to the Gospel of Jesus Christ, and acknowledgeth him the Saviour, whom God did promise." Now the question is, Whether the dissenting parties, in this last religion, be so far (not in opinion, but in the object) differing, as that there is no hope of reconciliation; and, the one part only, hath but the privilege, to be termed the Church? For the matter of reconcilement, it is no business, which lieth within the compass of this labour; and, whether, and how it may be done, we are willing to refer it to the judgments of men who have better ability to decide the cause. A book in Latin was published, in the first beginning of these bitter contentions, without name, bearing the title, "Of the Duty of a godly Man;" but since, Bellarmine saith, that the Author was one George Cassander; this book persuading that Princes ought to make an agreement betwixt the Catholics, the Lutherans, and Calvinists, as he terms them; which, whilst they cannot find out the means to perform, they should permit to all men their several Religions so that they held both the Scripture and the Apostles' Creed: for all (saith he) are the true members of the Church, howsoever in particular doctrines, they seem to differ.† This book was book was first confuted by Calvin, on the one side, and then by one John Hessels of Lovaine, on the other side; that all the world might see, how loath both sides were, to be made friends. This hath since been esteemed by others, a labour, much like to those pacificants in the Emperor Zeno his time,‡ or the heresy of Apelles, who held, as Eusebius writeth, that it was needless to discuss the particulars of our faith, and

---

* Optatus, cont. Parmen. lib. ii. epist. 166. et Ruffin. lib. x. cap. 5.
†Greg. lib. iv. epist. 32.   ‡ Evag. lib. iii. cap. 14, 30.

64

sufficient only to believe in Christ crucified.§ But lest any man should think that our contentions were but in smaller points, and the difference not great, both sides have charged the other with heresies (if not infidelities), nay even such as quite overthrow the principal foundation of our Christian faith. How truly both have dealt, those that are learned can best judge; but I am sure that in the greatest differences there are great mistakings, which if they were not, it is like their dissensions had been much less. Now for the second, Whether both parts may be called the Church? This is that which concerneth the Cause that we have in hand. The Church of England confesseth, that "the Church of Christ, is a company of faithful people, among whom the pure Word of God is preached, and the Sacraments rightly administered according to Christ's Institution;"* so that, as our reverend Fathers say, "without Christ there is no Church;" and that those particular Churches are more perfect which in their religious worship, have less failed in both these: now, when enemies become judges, sentences are often partial, and each side with bitterness of terms, doth condemn other; whilst neither part is willing to confess their error, or amend themselves. We have not suffered the contemptible revilings of the Church of Rome, without telling her aloud, That her faults are not so few as she imagineth; that her chastity and purity are not so great, that she need to boast; and, That if she will needs be proud and confidently strive to be the chief and the only Church, we must tell her in zeal, that what she was, she is not; that pride and prosperity have corrupted her, as other Churches. This though we speak out of zeal, seeing her faults, and knowing her contempt of us; yet out of judgment, we say (which Master Hooker doth) that "with Rome we dare not communicate, concerning sundry her gross and grievous abominations; yet touching those main parts of Christian truth, wherein they constantly still persist, we gladly acknowledge them to be of the family of Jesus Christ:"‡ therefore, "we hope that to reform ourselves, if at any time we have done

---

† De Officio Pii Viri, Tom. I. de Eccl. lib. iii. cap 19.   ‡ Euseb. Hist. lib. v. cap. 12.
§ Art. XIX. de Eccl.

amiss, is not to sever ourselves from the Church we were before; in the Church we were, and we are so still;"§ as also we say, that they of Rome, notwithstanding their manifold defects, are "to be held and reputed a part of the house of God; a limb of the visible church of Christ." This is that whereat your hot spirits have taken offence; speaking out of the same ignorant zeal against our Church, as ye wish our Church to speak against the Church of Rome; accounting us for perfection of a Church, as far short of you, as Rome is of us; or yourselves of the Angels that are in heaven; and therefore you affirm that our Statute congregations of England, are no true Christian churches. Which error, as you have at last been from an unresistible wisdom taught how to recant,¶ so no doubt, at length upon better advice, you will learn, in judgment, how to censure of the Church of Rome. And yet mistake me not, to give her her due, is not to grant more than she ought to challenge; nor, to account her a part of the Church, is not to affirm that she is absolutely perfect. There is no one word, that from the variety of acceptation, hath bred greater difference, in the Church of God, than the word CHURCH. Sometimes, it is taken for any Assembly;* sometimes for a faithful and religious Assembly; and then it sometimes noteth out the whole body of the elect in all ages, times, and places, both in heaven and earth; and only them. So it is in the Article of our Faith, "I believe the Catholic Church," that is, all those who are, or shall be saved, both angels and men; so it is taken in that speech of our Saviour, "Upon this rock will I build my Church,"†† that is, the whole Catholic Church. Sometimes it is taken for that part only which is in heaven: as when it is said, that the Church is "without spot, or wrinkle;" which can be verified of no part (whatsoever the Anabaptists dream) but of that which triumpheth. Sometimes it is taken for that *part* of the Catholic church, which is militant, "that thou mayst know how thou oughtest to behave thyself in the house of God which is the Church of the living God; the pillar and ground of truth;§ So, "fear came upon all the Church."‖

---

§ Preface against Dr. Bancroft.   *Psalm xxvi. 5. "Ecclesia malignantium."
†† Matt. xvi. 18.   ‡ Eph. v. 27.   ‖ Acts v. 11.

66

Sometimes it is taken for the pastors and governors only of the Church, as when it is said, "Tell the Church,"¶ that is, the heads and governors of the Church. Sometimes for the people, "Take heed therefore unto yourselves, and to all the flock, whereof the Holy Ghost hath made you overseers, to feed the Church of God, which he hath purchased with that his own blood."* Sometimes for particular Churches, professing the doctrine and religion of Christ: as, "To the Angel of the Church of Ephesus;"† so we say, The Church of Rome; The Church of Corinth; The Church of England. Now, from the mistaking of this word CHURCH, doubtless much harm and needless contentions have come unto the Church of Christ. For in the first great contention (Of what persons the Church consisteth?) in my opinion *we* dispute of one Church, namely, the true Catholic, all which must be saved; *they* dispute of the Visible, wherein are hypocrites also. So that the reasons that are brought on both sides, are smally to the purpose, seeing both sides directly mistake the question. Thus, in the judgment of those of the Church of Rome, persons excommunicate (though unjustly) are cut off from the particular Church, but not from the Catholic; excommunication being only, the censure of a particular Church: Therefore (saith our Saviour Christ) "many are called" (with an external calling to the society of the visible Church) "but few are chosen; ‡ that is, to the Catholic. For though both be a fold, yet of the visible Church (saith St. Austin) "In the Church there are many wolves, and out of the Church there are many sheep; but in the Catholic, without any other mixture are sheep only." Now visible and invisible maketh, not two Churches; but the divers estate and condition of one and the same Church. Hence cometh it to pass, that in this question, of the Visibility of the Church, there is the like mistaking as in the former; for they of Rome say, we have this distinction because our Church hath not been always visible; but we say, if our Church had been as glorious and as famous, as any Church in the world, we would have accounted the Catholic Church invisible: which (no doubt of it) they of Rome do, understanding (Catholic and

* Acts xx. 28   § 1 Tim. iii. 15.   ¶Matt. xvii. 17.
† Rev. ii. 1.   ‡ Matt. xxii. 11.

Visible) as we mean. For "the Church of Christ, which we properly term his mystical body, can be but one; neither can that one be sensibly discerned by any man; inasmuch as the parts thereof are some in heaven already with Christ, and the rest that are on earth, (albeit their natural persons be visible) yet we cannot discern under this property whereby they are truly and infallibly of that body; only our minds by internal conceit, are able to apprehend that such a real body there is, a body collective, (because it containeth a huge multitude) a body mystical, (because the mystery of their conjunction is removed altogether from sense). Whatsoever we read in Scripture concerning the endless love and the saving mercy which God shewed towards his Church, the only proper subject thereof is this Church. They who are of this Society have such marks and notes of distinction from all others, as are not subject* unto our sense; only unto God who seeth their hearts and understandeth all their secret cogitations, unto him, they are clear and manifest. In the eye of God, they are against Christ, that are not truly and sincerely with him; in our eyes, they must be received as with Christ, that are not to outward shew, against him; to him they seem such as they are, but of us they must be taken for such as they seem. All men knew Nathaniel to be an Israelite, but our Saviour, piercing deeper, giveth further testimony of him than men could have done with such certainty as he did; 'behold indeed an Israelite, in whom is no guile.'† Now as those everlasting promises of love, mercy, and blessedness, belong to the mystical Church; even so on the other side, when we read of any duty, which the Church of God is bound unto, the Church whom this doth concern is a sensible known company; and this visible Church in like sort is but one, continued from the first beginning of the world to the last end: which company, being divided into two parts, the one before, the other since the coming of Christ; that part which since the coming partly hath embraced and partly shall hereafter embrace the Christian Religion, we term as by a proper name, the Church of Christ. For all make but one body,* the unity of which visible Body and the

---

* [*Al.* "object," *sic* Hooker.]   † John i. 47.

Church of Christ consisteth in that uniformity which all several persons thereunto belonging have, by reason of that 'one Lord,' whose servants they all profess themselves to be; that 'one Faith,' which they all acknowledge; that 'one Baptism,' wherewith they are all received into the Church. As for those virtues that belong unto moral righteousness and honesty of life, we do not speak of them, because they are not proper unto Christian men, as they are Christian, but do concern them, as they are men. True it is, the want of these virtues, excludeth from salvation; so doth much more the absence of inward belief of heart; so doth despair and lack of hope; so emptiness of Christian love and charity; but we speak now, of the visible Church, whose Children are signed with this mark, 'One Lord, one Faith, one Baptism.' In whomsoever these things are, the Church doth acknowledge them for her children; them only she holdeth for aliens and strangers, in whom these things are not found. For want of these, it is that Saracens, Jews, and Infidels are excluded out of the bounds of the Church; others we may not (though you do) deny to be of the visible Church, as long as these things are not wanting in them. For apparent it is, that all men are of necessity either Christians or not Christians; if by external profession they be Christians, then are they of the visible Church of Christ; and Christians by external profession they are all, whose mark of recognizance hath in it those things which we have mentioned: yea although they be impious Idolaters, wicked Heretics, persons excommunicable, such as we deny not to be even the limbs of Satan, as long as they continue such. Is it then possible (say you) that the self-same men should belong both to the synagogue of Satan, and to the Church of Christ? Unto that Church, which is his mystical body, not possible; because that body consisteth of none but only true Israelites; true sons of Abraham, true servants and Saints of God. Howbeit of the visible body and Church of Christ, those may be, and oftentimes are, in respect of the main parts of their outward profession, who in regard of their inward disposition of mind, yea, of external conversation, yea, even of some parts of their

---

* Ephes. ii. 16

very profession, are most worthily both hateful in the sight of God himself, and in the eyes of the sounder parts of the visible Church, most execrable. From hence have proceeded those bitter speeches, wherewith many of our reverend Fathers have censured the Church of Rome: as also those violent courses and unseemly, which they have hitherto used against us. Therefore our Saviour compareth the kingdom of heaven, to a net,† whereunto all that cometh neither is nor seemeth fish; his Church he compareth to a field,* where tares manifestly known and seen by all men, do grow intermingled with good corn; and so shall continue till the final consummation of the world. God hath had ever, and ever shall have, some Church visible upon earth. But for lack of diligent observing the difference, first betwixt the Church of God mystical and visible; then between the visible sound and corrupted, sometimes more, sometimes less, the oversights are neither few nor light that have been committed: This deceiveth them, and nothing else, who think that in the time of the first world, the family of Noah did contain all that were of the visible Church of God. From hence it grew, and from no other cause in the world, that the African bishops in the Council of Carthage, knowing how the administration of Baptism belongeth only to the Church of Christ, and supposing that Heretics, which were apparently severed from the sound believing church, could not possibly be of the Church of Jesus Christ, thought it utterly against reason, that Baptism administered by men of corrupt belief, should be accounted as a Sacrament. Some of the Fathers were earnest, especially St. Cyprian, in this point: (but I hope you have not yet proceeded so far). This opinion was afterwards both condemned by a better advised Council, and also revoked by the chiefest of the Authors thereof themselves:‡ And therefore as it is strange for any man to deny them of Rome to be of the Church; so I cannot but wonder, that they will ask where our Church was, before the birth of Martin Luther; as if any were of opinion that Luther did erect a new Church of Christ. No, the Church of Christ, which was from the beginning, is, and continueth

---

* Matt. xiii. 47.   † Matt. xiii. 24.   * In Conc. Nicen. vide Hieron. in Di. cont. Lucifer.

in substance the same unto the end; of which, all parts have not been always equally sincere and sound. In the days of Abia, it plainly appeareth that Judah was by many degrees more free from pollution than Israel: in St. Paul's time the integrity of Rome was famous; Corinth many ways reproved;† they of Galatia much more out of square: in John's time, Ephesus and Smyrna, in better state than Thyatira and Pergamos were; and yet all of them, no doubt, parts of the visible Church; so standeth the cause, betwixt Rome and us; so far as lawfully we may, we have held, and do hold fellowship with them; we acknowledge them to be of the family of Jesus Christ; and our hearty prayer unto God Almighty is, that being conjoined, so far forth with them, they may at length, if it be his will, so yield to frame and reform themselves, that no distraction remain in any thing, but that we all may 'with one heart and one mouth glorify God, the Father of our Lord and Saviour, whose Church we are.'‡ As there are, which make the Church of Rome no Church at all, utterly; so we have them amongst us, who under pretence of imagined corruptions in our discipline, do give even as hard a judgment of the Church of England itself. But whatsoever either the one sort, or the other teach, we must acknowledge, even Heretics themselves, to be (though a maimed part) yet a part of the visible Church. For as to baptize is a proper action, belonging unto none but the Church of Christ, which is true in the Church of Rome (howsoever some Anabaptists account it but a mockery) so if an Infidel should pursue to death an Heretic, professing Christianity, only for Christian profession' sake, could the Church deny him the honour of martyrdom? Yet this honour all men know to be proper unto the Church; and therefore where the Fathers make opposition betwixt the visible Church, and heretical companies (as oftentimes they do) they are to be construed, as separating Heretics, not altogether from the company of believers, but from the fellowship of sound Believers: for where professed *unbelief* is, there can be no visible Church of Christ; there may be where sound belief wanteth. Infidels being clean without the Church deny directly, and utterly reject, the very

---

† 2 Cor. xiii. 2.   ‡ [Rom. xv. 6. with Heb. iii. 6.]

principles of Christianity; which Heretics embrace, and err only in misconstruction. And therefore it is strange that you dare affirm;† the Turk to hold any part of the Christian faith, or to be in that respect comparable to the Church of Rome: for "that which separateth utterly, that which cutteth off clean from the visible Church of Christ, is," as Master Hooker saith, "plain Apostasy; direct denial, utter rejection of the whole Christian Faith, as far as the same is professedly different, from Infidelity. Heretics, as touching those points of doctrine wherein they fail; Schismatics, as touching the quarrels for which, or the duties wherein they divide themselves from their brethren; loose, licentious, and wicked persons, as touching their several offences or crimes, have all forsaken the true Church of God; the Church which is sound and sincere in the doctrine that they corrupt: the Church that keepeth the bond of unity which they violate; the Church that walketh in the laws of righteousness which they transgress; this very true Church of Christ, they have left, howbeit not altogether left, nor forsaken simply the Church, upon the main foundations whereof, they continue built, notwithstanding these breaches, whereby they are rent at the top asunder." But peradventure you will say, Why then do we refuse to communicate with the Church of Rome, more than Zachary, Elizabeth, Anna, and others, did with the High Priests; corruptions being in both, and both remaining parts of the Church of God? I answer, That in the time of our Saviour Christ, the synagogue of the Jews although it was not in regard of the High Priests and chief Doctors, in all respects, the true visible Church; yet in some sort, it was; because the remainders of religion were left, and the worship instituted of God himself was not wholly taken away: so with the Papists we would not be afraid to communicate, in our Liturgy, if it were not in respect of their superstitious order and some prayers which are idolatrous, for which we have some reasons as yet, to doubt that they have no warrant. We must all of us be joined to the true Church, else we cannot be saved; that is to the catholic, not the visible: for, doubtless, a man may be saved that liveth not in any particular Church; or, that is excommunicated from all: yet we say, thus much, That we must join ourselves to some particular Church, if we will be saved; with this twofold caution, If such a Church be known unto us; or, if it be possible to join unto it. Wherein, because every particular may err yet none absolutely exclude from salvation, all men have reason to join with that that is most sound. This then were the fittest point to be discussed with moderation and learning, That seeing all Churches have some unsound parts in them, which Church is to be reputed at this day the soundest of all the rest? Doubtless the Church of Rome was once a light to all the Churches of the world;* but through the corruptions of some, those diseases have somewhat infected the Church which now, to the sorrow of Christendom, like a canker, or leprosy, have enlarged themselves. As there is a contention when Adam fell; so, histories vary, when this defection began. Some make five or six hundred years to be the continuance of her sound estate; some, three hundred; some, to err even from the Apostles' time. Doubtless in the Apostles' time, there were heretics in the Church; the Nicolaitans, Simon Magus, Cerinthus, and others. Eusebius reporteth out of Egesippus, That although as long as the Apostles lived, the Church did remain a pure virgin; yet after those times, immediately, errors crept into the Church.‡ Clemens Alexandrinus, to confirm that there was corruption of doctrine presently after the Apostles' time, allegeth the proverb, "There are few sons like their fathers." Socrates saith of the Church of Rome and Alexandria (the most famous Churches in the Apostles' time), That about the year 430, the Roman and Alexandrian Bishops, leaving their sacred function, were degenerate to a secular rule or dominion. Yet we say not, that all before Gregory were sound, nor all after, corrupt: yet their errors grew on by little and little, even from those men whose reverend names gave warrant to what they held; they thinking nothing less than by those means, to have corrupted the Church. But she may, when it pleaseth God, recover her former soundness again: if we had but so much care of them, as they seem to have of us: or that all sides, peaceably, with indifferency, would admit the true use of a General Council. But let their errors be as they are; we leave them to be reproved by those

---

* Rom. i. 8.   † Calvin. Melanet.   ‡ Lib. iii. cap. 32.

whom that business doth concern, and to be judged by the Searcher of all hearts: yet for all that, we affirm them to be *parts* of the Church of Christ; and, that those that live and die in that Church, may not withstanding be saved. Of those who are of a contrary opinion in a good meaning, I say with Lactantius, "With how good a meaning these poor souls do evil!"* To conclude, lest you should think Master Hooker to be "arrogant and presumptuous to make himself (as you say) the only Rabbi;"† know that he hath said nothing which that honourable Frenchman of worthy memory ‡ hath not said before, with great wisdom, moderation, and learning. But if you cannot be resolved without a miracle, as you scoffingly seem to desire, we can but in our prayers recommend your weakness to the God of all power, and the fountain of all light.

---

§ Inst. lib. v. cap. 19. "O quam honesta voluntate miseri errant."
¶ In his Treatise of the Church, chap. 2

ARTICLE XII.

OF PREACHING

How hard it is for those, who are in love with themselves, to carry a well tempered indifferency betwixt that which they out of ignorance perform, and others out of judgment avoid; this Article alone, may serve as evidence sufficient to persuade all. For, even in the matter of greatest use unto God's Church (the dispensation of the Word of Life), a vehement dislike of those things which they cannot attain, hath wrought too violent an opposition, for the overthrow of that course which learning and truth have held not to be the weakest means to support the same. Hence cometh it to pass, that whilst all grant the Word to be powerful and effectual, some, think this is only true, of the Word preached; which otherwise hath small virtue, except it be in sermons, and those sermons only to have this power, which are of their own making. Causing the Holy Ghost, whose strength is perfected in weakness,* to be necessarily tied to a defect of all outward ornaments; as though that Almighty power upon whomever excellency depends, even in the weakest means, were of less authority, or less power, when the means which he useth were more excellent: thus depriving the Church of variety of gifts, who, out of obedience and humility, hath learned how to profit by all. But, as to tie the power of converting sinners to that which is eloquently strong in human wisdom were a thing not safe,

---

* 2 Cor. xii. 9.

76

and injurious to the Church; so, to be too earnest against all outward ornaments, through an affectation of pure simplicity, is an error no less dangerous than the former was. For seeing those that teach are not all either capable or furnished with the same gifts; and that, continually, there is no less variety in those that hear; it is the wisdom and discretion of the Church, for a better attainment of a more perfect estate, to learn with thankfulness and reverence how to profit by all. For as it is impossible that any one form of Teaching should please or persuade all men (a prerogative which was not granted to the first and best sermons), whose excellency was that they converted "many," but not all;* so the rest who yet are not but must be converted, are to expect (though not with curiosity to affect) a variety for the manner even of that which in substance and end is but merely one. For the mystical body, as it is full of variety and diversity in his [*its*] parts, yet, in itself, but one; so the working is manifold and different, though the beginning and the end, God's power, and his glory, be in truth, to and for all men, but one. For sometimes the Word, by being read, proposeth and preacheth itself to the hearer; sometimes they deliver it whom, privately, zeal and piety moveth to be instructors of others by conference: sometimes of them it is taught, whom the Church hath called to the public either reading thereof, or interpreting; and by them, after a most divers manner, but all tending to one end, for which God hath made his visible Church to be that "congregation of faithful people, wherein the pure Word of God is preached:"† so that in this respect we refuse not, to make the Preaching of the Word (taking the word Preaching for all manner of teaching) to be an essential note of the Church. For doubtless, in that parable of the sower,* by you alleged,‡ we mislike not much the interpretation of that Reverend Bishop which you bring forth, as opposite to Master Hooker; saying, "God is the husbandman, the Preachers of the Word are the seed sowers, the seed is the Word of God, the ground is the hearts of men;" and yet St. Austin differeth a little from this exposition, where he saith, The sower is God, and

---

† Acts iv. 4.   * [Art. XIX.]   † Matt. xiii. 3.

I, because he soweth, what am I but the seedman's basket?¶ Which even the meanest
Christian no doubt is, though never called to the office of Preaching, if he can, by
private conference, exhort and instruct out of holy Scripture: which as it is an act of
less honour and profit, than the Preaching of those that are worthily called to that
office; so even in their sermons that are called, there is no man but must
acknowledge, a manifold, and apparent difference. For "seeing speech" (as Master
Hooker saith; which you mislike) "is the very image whereby the mind and soul of
the speaker conveyeth itself into the bosom of him that heareth; we cannot choose but
see great reason wherefore the Word that proceeded from God (who is in himself
very truth and life) should be (as the Apostle to the Hebrews noteth) lively, and
mighty in operation, "sharper than any two-edged sword."* Now, to make our
Sermons that strong and forcible Word, is to impart the most peculiar glory of the
Word of God, unto that which is not his Word. For, touching our Sermons, that
which giveth them their very being, is the will [*wit*] of man, and therefore they
oftentimes accordingly taste too much of that over corrupt fountain from which they
come." For even the best of our Sermons (and in Sermons there is an infinite
difference) howsoever they oftentimes have a singular blessing, and that the
Scripture, the pure Word of God, is the text and the ground of the speech; yet the rest
of the discourse, which is sometimes two or three hours long, (a time too long for
most preachers to speak pertinently) is but the paraphrastical enlarging of the same
text, together with those fit exhortations and applications, which the learning of the
Preacher is able to furnish himself withal, and his discretion shall think fit for that
auditory to which he speaketh. And therefore, as to equalize "every declamation or
oration in Schools," to them, is to wrong sermons; so to make even the best Sermons
equal to the Scripture, must be, in apparent reason, a great wrong to that which is
immediately God's own word; whereunto, though the best preach agreeably, yet the
Sermons of none, since the Apostles' time, are or ought to be esteemed of equal

§ Bishop of Lincol. 1st. Serm. upon Matt. xiii.   ¶Cophinus Seminantis."
*Heb. iv. 12.

authority with the holy Scripture and yet, we are not afraid to ascribe unto them, that blessing from above, to convert, reform, and strengthen, which no "eloquence, wisdom, learning, policy, and power of the world," is able to match. Neither is there contrariety in this, that we that are the Preachers are sent as the Apostles were, in respect of our calling from God; and yet, that the learning and wit of man giveth the very being unto that we teach. Unless (which some overboldly do) you think it unlawful to use either learning or wit in making of Sermons: as though all other helps, purchased with great cost and infinite labour, together with a natural ability, all perfected in those excellent fountains of all learning, the Universities, were to be reflected as wholly unprofitable in this business. Neither doth Master Hooker, nor any other of judgment, say (which you seem to infer) That a man by natural wit, without a supernatural light from the Scripture, is able to utter those mysteries as he ought; which doubtless being a great fault, is rather the error of those who preach most and yet use least helps of learning or wit for that they utter. Wherein it must needs seem strange, that they ever understanding by the Word, the word preached, whereunto they ascribe vital operation; yet they perform this with such negligence, that they come rashly unfurnished to so great a business; and scarce attentively weigh the dangerous sequel of this construction. Doubtless, our Sermons, even the best, either for sound knowledge, or pure zeal, are not God's Word in the same manner that the Sermons of the Prophets were; no, they are but ambiguously termed his Word, because his Word is commonly the subject whereof they treat, and must be the rule whereby they are framed. Yet Sermons have sundry peculiar and proper virtues, such as no other way of Teaching besides hath: aptness, to follow particular occasions presently growing; to put life into words by countenance, voice, and gesture; to prevail mightily in the sudden affections of men; these, and such like, are those excellent prerogatives which some few may challenge who worthily deserve the name to be called Preachers. We reject not (as of no use at all in the Church) even the virtuous labours of meaner men, who come far short of the perfection of these few; but earnestly wish the Governors of our Church, for fit employment and maintenance, to respect both: and they, laying aside all comparisons, equally to labour to further that work which, by a blessing from above, knoweth how to profit by the labours of all. It seemeth, by that which you allege, that only such Sermons have their being, from the wit of man, which "curiously bring into the Pulpit, Poets, Philosophers, Rhetoricians, Physicians, Schoolmen," and other human learning; which "the Reverend Fathers," say you, "and more staid divines, are wary to avoid." In this speech of yours, in my opinion, there are two faults. The first, a particular unjust censure of the Fathers, whether you mean, the holy Fathers of the Church, as St. Austin, St. Ambrose, St. Gregory, St. Bernard, and the rest; or, those reverend Fathers which do live at this day; all which, whilst you seek to commend, directly you dispraise; accounting them to avoid all human learning, and that their Sermons have not their being from the wit of man: which doubtless is false, seeing they excel by infinite degrees, the Sermons of many others which are framed by neither. The second fault, is a general taxation of all those who any way furnish their Sermons with human learning. You may, peradventure, be able to give good direction in other points, but surely in framing of a Preacher, or making of a Sermon, you are much deceived: for I can never persuade myself, that the exactest industry that man can use is unlawful or unnecessary in this work; for sometimes we are to deal with those whose opinions are not easily confuted without human learning, nor their attention gained without wit, nor their affections persuaded without eloquence; where to come unfurnished, and leave the workings, without means, to Him who giveth a power and a blessing to the means we use, is all one to appoint him what means are fittest, or to enjoin him to work without means at all: which, though that Almighty power can do, yet then to refuse them when they are provided, or not to furnish us with as much as we can of the best that he hath provided, it argueth our unthankfulness and our want of choice. This made (when Celsus, Julian, and Porphyry, had written against us) the holy Fathers to confute them with all variety of human learning; that thus the enemies of that Truth which we teach, may say with Julian, We are struck through with our own weapons.* This was the happiness of Epiphanius (which I wish were common to all Preachers) That his writings were read of the learned, for the matter; of the simple, for the words. Thus we should not doubt but to win an attention from all; nay, even for the true discharging of this business, there is a necessary use of Grammar, to teach the original and propriety of words; of Logic, to discern ambiguities; of Rhetoric, for ornament (a good tale being much better when it is well told); of Philosophy, for the unfolding the true nature of causes, the ignorance whereof hath brought much error in expounding the holy Scriptures; of History, for the computation of times; in one word, of all human learning, which, like the spoils of Egypt, we have recovered from the unjust owners; accounting it no more disgrace to be accused of eloquence, wit, or human learning, than St. Austin did by Petilian, to be termed Tertullus the Orator. There be that account incivility of manners, and rusticity of speech, as St. Jerome speaketh, true holiness.† But it is not fit, that those that are toothless should envy the teeth of others; or those that are moles, repine that others see (as the same Father admonisheth Calphurnius).‡ It hath been a trouble of some of our best and most excellent Preachers, that they have been enforced, after their wearisome toiling and unregarded pains, to give a reason and make a defence (as though they had committed a fault) for the use of that for which, in true estimation, they ought to have reaped much praise. And therefore saith one (whom I dare oppose, for eloquence and judgment, against the best in that great city § of the contrary faction), "I am not of opinion with those men who think that all secular and profane learning should be abandoned from the lips of the Preacher; and, that whether he teach, or exhort, he is of necessity to tie himself to the sentence and phrase of only Scripture. Good is good, wheresoever I find it."‖ Upon a withered and fruitless stalk, saith St. Austin, a grape sometimes may hang; shall I refuse the

---

* "Propriis pennis configimur."   ‡ Epist. ad Rom.
§ London.   ‖ M. King upon Jonas, p. 541.

grape because the stalk is fruitless and withered?¶ There is not any knowledge of learning to be despised, seeing that all science whatsoever is in the nature and kind of good things; rather, those that despise it, we must repute rude and unprofitable altogether, who would be glad that all men were ignorant that their own ignorance, lying in the common heap, might not be espied. And St. Austin in another place,* saith, Eloquence is not evil, but a sophistical malignant profession, proposing to itself, not as it meaneth, but either of contention, or for commodity' sake, to speak for all things and against all things. What were more profitable, than the eloquence of Donatus, Parmenian, and others of your sect, if it ran with as free a stream, for the peace, unity, truth, and love of Christ, as it floweth against it? For else, it is a venomous eloquence, as St. Cyprian wrote of the eloquence of Novatus;† I know there is much amiss, both in matter, and in the use of profane learning; but this we are sure, if we bring it to the Scripture, if it be faulty, it is condemned; if wholesome, it is there confirmed. And I see no reason, that any man should be bold to offer his own inventions and conceits to the world, when he findeth such in the Fathers and others, as cannot be amended. I am sorry that the Learned of any sort (as my Author saith) that hath but borne a book, should dispraise Learning; she hath enemies enough abroad, though she be justified by her children. It is fitter that Wisdom be beaten by fools, than by those who ought to be esteemed wise; above all other places a blow given in the Pulpit against Learning (a fault too common) leaveth a scar in the face of Knowledge which cannot easily be cured. It calleth in question the teaching of others, as if they fed the people with acorns and husks, not bread; or because they gather the Truth out of human Authors, they contemned the Authority of the holy Scriptures. Doubtless, it is sometime vanity in those that preach, and itching in those that hear, and a thing not tolerable, or allowable in either; but where it is otherwise, let not a rash conclusion without proof (as though it were young men's faults) be admitted against good Learning. If Asclepiodorus will draw with a coal or chalk

† Ad Marcell. epist. 102.   ¶ De Baptis. cont. Donat. lib. vi. c. 2.
* Advers. Cresco. lib. i. cap. 1.

alone, I judge him not; if others will paint with colours, neither let them be judged: for those, that are wise and humble in the Church know how, with discretion, to make use of all; and yet, not all of the like authority. For doctrines derived, exhortations deducted, interpretations agreeable, are not the very Word of God, but that only which is in the original text, or truly translated; and yet we call those Sermons, though improperly, the Word of God. To conclude this point; as our Church hath many excellent Preachers, which we wish by good encouragement may increase; so it is too presumptuous a labour for any to prescribe one form necessary to all. But I could wish that all were like him whom you accuse, or like one Marianus Genazanensis, whom Angelus Politianus doth excellently describe,† in my opinion an excellent pattern of a reverend Divine.

---

* Epist. ad. Cornel.   † Epist. Tristano Chalco. lib. iv. epist. 6.

ARTICLE XIII.

OF THE MINISTER'S OFFICE

In the actions of this life, whether spiritual or temporal, God and man give their approbation in a diverse manner; the one, looketh only at the thing done; the other, at the mind and disposition of the doer. And therefore, the same things from divers parties are not of the same nor of like value: nay, that which is from sincerity, a worship, is from hypocrisy, a sin: and the defects, which outwardly the manner of doing disproveth, the sincerity oftentimes in the mind of the doer, acquitteth. In the eye of man, it is sometimes a fault which is no sin; and, in the eye of God, a sin which, in the eye of man, was no fault. So that according to laws which principally respect the heart of man, works of Religion being not religiously performed, cannot morally be perfect. Baptism, as an Ecclesiastical work, is for the manner of performance ordered by divers ecclesiastical laws, providing, that as the sacrament itself is a gift of no mean worth; so the ministry thereof might, in all circumstances, appear to be a function of no small regard. The Ministry of the things divine, is a function which as God did himself institute, so neither may men undertake the same but by authority and power given them in lawful manner. That God, which is no way deficient or wanting unto man in necessaries, and hath therefore given us the light of his heavenly Truth, because without that inestimable benefit we must needs have wandered in darkness, to our endless perdition; and, who hath in the like abundance of mercies, ordained certain to attend upon the due execution of requisite parts, and offices, therein prescribed, for the good of the whole world; which men, thereunto assigned, do hold their authority from him, whether they be such, as himself immediately, or else the Church in his name, investeth; it being neither possible, for all, nor for every man without distinction convenient, to take upon him a charge of so great importance: and therefore very fitly, "the Church of England affirmeth, that It is not lawful for any one to take to himself the Office of Preaching publicly, or administering the Sacraments in the Church, except he be first lawfully called to these things:"* For God who hath reserved, even from the first beginning of the world until the end thereof, a Church unto himself upon earth; against which, the gates of hell shall not prevail; hath likewise appointed, a perpetual Ministry for the service therein; which though for outward calling hath not been ever the same, yet continually it was limited, in those bounds, as a thing most unmeet and unlawful for any man to undertake that was not called. For as it is God's infinite mercy, when he could either save us without the Ministry of any, or by the Ministry of Angels; yet then, to honour man, with this dignity to make him a coadjutor, dispenser, and co-helper in so great a work, so it is his wisdom to appoint, both for the avoiding of confusion and unfitness, such persons as are truly allotted to so honourable an office; which neither before, under, nor after the Law, was ever lawful without any calling to undertake. The enemies to this religious order of the Church, have been certain lovers of confusion which, under pretence of the calling of the Spirit, have overboldly intruded themselves into those holy functions for which, lawfully, they had never warrant. Such were the Enthusiasts, Anabaptists, Schwenkfeldians; who being enemies to all order, under pretence of a calling from the Holy Ghost, which others wanted, have made a passage contrary to that restraint of the Apostle, "Let no man take upon him that honour to himself, but he that is called of God,"** without expectation of lawful warrant, to those duties, that in the Church are greatest: for in the time before the Law, it was not permitted to take the office of Priesthood, unless

---

* Eccl. Ang. Art. XXIII.   ** Heb. v. 4.

he either were or had the prerogative of the eldest brother. This was for the sin of Reuben derived to the tribe of Levi; first, for their zeal in that great idolatry; and was after confirmed unto him, in the sedition of Corah: and yet not to all of that family, either to serve in that tabernacle,† or to teach throughout all Israel. Neither were all ages equally fit unto this calling; it being neither lawful before five-and-twenty, nor after fifty, to be admitted to it.‡ As also, those that were admitted had a special consecration, for a personal difference from the rest of that family, to let them understand that although they, and only they of that tribe, were to be employed in those functions, yet it was not lawful to undertake it, without a calling:§ this, afterward, when better notes of eminency gave that allowance which, before, birth did, was with greater reverence to be expected, and to be observed with a greater care, by those whom the Church had invested with Authority to call unto that charge. To these persons, because God imparted power over his mystical body, which is the society of souls, and over that natural which is himself, for the knitting of both in one (a work which antiquity doth call the making of Christ's body), the same power is in such not amiss both termed a kind of mark or Character, and acknowledged to be indelible.* "For Ministerial Power is a mark of separation, because it severeth them that have it from other men, and maketh them a special Order, consecrated unto the service of the Most High in things wherewith others may not meddle. Their difference, therefore, from other men is in that they are a distinct Order:" and I call it indelible, because "they which have once received this Power," as Master Hooker saith, "may not think to put it off and on like a cloak, as the weather serveth, to take it, reject and resume it as oft as themselves list; of which profane and impious contempt these latter times have yielded (as of all other kinds of iniquity and apostasy) strange examples. But let them know, which put their hands to this plough, that once consecrated unto God, they are made his peculiar inheritance for ever. Suspensions may stop, and degradations utterly cut off, the use or exercise of Power

---

** Levit. xxi. 21. ‡Numb. viii. 24, 25. § Exod. xxix. Levit. viii. Numb. viii.

given; but voluntarily it is not in the power of man to separate and pull asunder what God by his authority coupleth: neither need there a Reordination for such as were consecrated by the Church, in corrupter times; for "out of men endued with gifts of the Spirit, the Church chose her Ministers, unto whom was given Ecclesiastical Power by Ordination," which they could neither assume nor reject at their own pleasure. Of these, without doubt the "Apostolic Churches, did acknowledge but three degrees at the first; Apostles (instead whereof, are now Bishops), Presbyters, and Deacons; for there is an error (as Master Hooker saith) which beguileth many, who much entangle both themselves and others, by not distinguishing Services, Offices, and Orders Ecclesiastical; the first of which three, and in part the second, may be executed by the Laity,‡ whereas none have, or can have the third, namely, 'Order,' but the Clergy. Catechists, Exorcists, Readers, Singers, and the rest of like sort, if the nature only of their labour and pains be considered, may in that respect seem clergymen; even as the Fathers for that cause term them usually Clerks; as also in regard of the end whereunto they were trained up, which was to enter into Orders when years and experience should make them able, notwithstanding, inasmuch as they in no way differed from others of the Laity longer than during that work of Service, which at any time they might give over, being thereunto but admitted, not tied by irrevocable Ordination, we find them always exactly severed from that body, whereof those three before-rehearsed Orders alone are natural parts. This will appear more fully (howsoever you mislike it) if we consider but a little, those services, and duties, about which they were employed. The first were Door-keepers,† (for we omit the first tonsor, which was not any order but a preparation) whose office was, as Master Calvin noteth, to open and to shut the doors of the temple,¶ we agree in this with the Church of Rome,§ our difference is, for the Ordination of them. The second were Readers, the duty of these, as Zanchy saith, was only to read the Bible, without any exposition, in a pulpit or place more eminent

---

‡ Ostiarii.   ¶ Instit. lib. iv. cap. iv. sect. 9. [et cap. 19. sect. 24.]

than the rest, so that, in the compass of a whole year, it was fully finished and read over: this was to make the people who could not read, more familiarly acquainted with the holy Scriptures. Of this duty, St. Cyprian in his Epistles, hath written most, as of one Aurelius, being made a Reader, of one Saturus, as also of Celerinus, which afterward was a Martyr.* The difference betwixt us, in this point, and the Church of Rome, is, that they make it a certain degree and Order, which Master Calvin doth not,** which, in my opinion, is no material difference, seeing undoubtedly the Church by special Ordination (without Ecclesiastical Order) appointed those whom she used in those places. The next were Exorcists, which did adjure those that were possessed with unclean spirits, but this was rather, doubtless, a peculiar gift, than any ordinary Office in God's Church.† The next were Disputers,§ which were appointed with all comers to defend the religion, against the heathen. The next were *Acolouthi*,‖ Attendants upon the Bishops, with whom these had their learning and reverend behaviour, that familiarity that they were thought fittest to succeed in the place of Bishops. This, as it was an employment of great respect, so it is retained in the Church of Rome at this day, with too mean a regard for so reverend a place. The next were Singers;¶ for it was thought unfit, that a Bishop, a Presbyter, or Deacon, should do this. The last which we will reckon, were the Catechists,** whose office was to teach children, and others converted, the sum of Christian doctrine.†† This duty was referred to learned men, sometimes Presbyters, Doctors, or Deacons, but not ever. For though Origen and Clemens were both Doctors and Catechists, in Alexandria, yet all that were Catechists, and so allowed to expound and teach the Scriptures, were not of necessity admitted to holy Orders:* and so, consequently, as the word is *properly* taken by Master Hooker, none of the Clergy. I say, properly,

¶ Epist. v. lib. ii. Epist. xxii. lib. iii. Epist. v. lib. iv.   † Inst. lib. iv. cap. 4. sect. 9.
‡ Exorcistæ. Cal. lib. iv. cap. 19. sect. 24. Zanch. in 4. Præcep. p. 688.
§ Disputatores.   ‖ Acolouthi.   ¶ Cantatores. Greg. in Regist. lib. iv. cap. 88.
** Catechista.   †† Gal. vi. 6.

88

for Clergy is a general name for all those, whose lot and portion is the Lord: More specially for those who are students in divinity and, after, are to enter into holy Orders. Of these, there were Colleges, after the Apostles, as before, Colleges of the Prophets. And out of these were taken such, as the Church (without Ecclesiastical ordination) used in those services which before are mentioned. Out of all which, it is most apparent that from the Clergy, in respect of Ministerial power, these are justly severed. This is that which you mislike, esteeming it a thing unfit, for any man to preach that hath not a Ministerial calling. Neither doth Master Hooker determine, how fit it is that this should be performed by men who are not entered into Orders, but, that this hath sometimes been the practice of the Church, howsoever now performed by men of another calling, there is no man of any reading can possibly doubt. Neither is the practice in some Colleges of Divines, at this day, altogether unlike; where men are admitted, even for exercise or trial, to interpret and expound the Scriptures, which are not as yet (but hereafter may be) consecrated to an Ecclesiastical Function. Now, whereas you scoff at the word *Character*, as if there were no stamp at all which made a difference betwixt the Clergy and the Laity, know, that where there is a change of estate, with an impossibility of return, there we have reason to account an indelible Character to be "imprinted." This saith the Church of Rome, is in Baptism, Confirmation, and Order.† Of the last of which, we only contend, at this time. For any thing that I read, Saint Austin was the first that used the word in this sense: and no doubt of it, in Baptism there is that Mark stamped upon us in that we are baptized, that there is a *passive* power, as the Schoolmen call it, which maketh a man, in time, fit to receive the rest which they call Sacraments, and without which;‖ they are truly accounted void. This form, figure, impression, or Character, is called "indelible," because that is not to be reiterated, from whence it cometh. The Character of Order, is an *active* power, as the Schoolmen speak, which giveth an ability, publicly, to administer the Sacraments

---

†Bell. Tom. II. p. 220.   ‡["Mark."]

unto those whom the Church hath esteemed fit. From whence proceedeth the second great exception which you have taken in this Article, namely, that Master Hooker seemeth to grant a liberty, as for Catechists to preach who are no Ministers; so also, for Women, in cases of some necessity, to Baptize; contrary, say you, both to that most Reverend Archbishop,§ and others,"who constantly affirm, That God, and well ordered Churches, forbid Women all dispensation of holy mysteries." We are not to dispute, what Laws give allowance to the performance of this office; nor, what care ought to make restraint from too usual a liberty of doing it without great necessity; seeing, weakness is commonly bold, and boldness a presumptuous intruder where it hath least cause. But this we say, which Mr. Hooker hath proved already, That Baptism by Women is truly Baptism; good and effectual to those that have it: neither do all those exceptions of sex, quality, insufficiency, or whatsoever, serve to frustrate such as the Church, of her indulgence, is willing to admit, from being partakers of so great a benefit. To make Women teachers in the House of God, were a gross absurdity, seeing the Apostle hath said, "I permit not a Woman to teach:"* and if any, from the same ground, exclude them from other public offices in the Church, we are not much against it. "But to women's Baptism, in private, by occasion of urgent necessity, the reasons that concern ordinary Baptism, in public, are no just prejudice; neither can we, by force thereof, disprove the practice of those Churches which ('necessity' requiring) allow Baptism, in private, to be administered by Women. We may not from Laws that prohibit any thing with restraint, conclude absolute, and unlimited prohibitions. For, even things Lawful are well prohibited, when there is fear lest they make the way to unlawful more easy; and it may be, the liberty of Baptism by Women at such times, doth sometimes embolden the rasher sort to do it where no such 'necessity' is. But whether of permission besides Law, or in presumption against Law, they do it (which now is no part of the question in hand), it is not hereby altogether frustrate, void, and as if it were never given."† True it is,

§ My Lord his Grace of Cant. Dr. Whitgift. p. 516.   * 1 Tim. ii. 12.   † "[Ministry," *sic* Hooker.]

90

that "seeing God, from whom men's several degrees and pre-eminences proceed, hath appointed them in his Church at whose hands his pleasure is that we should receive Baptism and all other public helps medicinable to the soul, perhaps, thereby the more to settle our hearts in the love of our Ghostly superiors; they have small cause to hope, that with him their voluntary services will be accepted, who thrust themselves into Functions, either above their capacity, or besides their place; and, overboldly inter-meddle with duties whereof no charge was ever given unto them." In which respect, if Laws forbid it to be done, yet therefore it is not unnecessarily void when it is done. For "many things are firm being done, which in part are done otherwise than positive rigour and strictness did require." Actions usurped, have often the same nature, which they have in others, although they yield not him that doth them the same comfort. What defects, then, are in this kind, they redound with restraint to the offender only; "the Grace of Baptism cometh, by donation, from God only. That God hath committed the mystery of Baptism unto special men, it is for Order's sake in his Church, and not to the intent that their Authority might give being, or add force to the Sacrament itself. Infants have right to Baptism, we all know; that they have it not by Lawful ministers, it is not their fault: Men's own faults are their own harms."¶ So then we conclude this point, with Master Hooker, that it is one thing to defend the fact for lawfulness in the doer (which few do) and another thing the fact being done, which no man hath reason to disallow; for though it is not lawful for Women to undertake that office to baptize, which peradventure belongs not unto them; yet the Baptism being done, we hold it lawful.

ARTICLE XIV.

OF THE SACRAMENTS.

It is not a thing less usual in the apprehension of truths, through the weakness of our understanding, to ascribe too little to that, which, in all reason, hath great virtue; than to allow overmuch to that, which hath no virtue at all. It fareth with men, in this kind, as it doth with some deceitful artificers; who bestow most art and outward additions where, inwardly there is least value, whilst they leave that altogether unfurnished, which is able to expose it to sale by his [*its*] own worth. It is our fault, no less violently, to extol what our fancies make us to account excellent, than to dispraise things truly commendable in their own nature, because only they have gained this disadvantage, To be disliked by us. So that whosoever maketh either praise or dispraise, to be a rule of judgment; or the judgment of some few, to be a sign of value; he, with like hazard, equally erreth in both. For times and places, violent circumstances of that which men say with or against, breed infinite variety of alterations where things are the same; and out of Commendation alone (a strange effect!) Dispraise, like a monster, doth spring up. It being cause sufficient, to distempered humours, vehemently to dislike only in this respect, That others do commend the same. Wherein the safest, and most charitable direction will be absolutely, in that violent opposition, to believe neither; but even from both, to derive a truth much sounder than that which either holdeth. From hence, hath it come to pass, that, whilst they of the Church of Rome have, peradventure, ascribed too much

92

to Works; some of us, too little; others, have set down an equality, dissenting from both. Thus, in the matter of the Sacraments, (things of greatest and most hidden virtue left unto the Church, for they are Mysteries) some, have been thought to derive that power to them which belongeth to God only; which, whilst others sought to avoid, they have even deprived them of that grace which God, doubtless in truth, hath bestowed upon them. In this kind, you are of opinion, that Mr. Hooker hath erred; who, as you imagine, hath ascribed to the Sacraments, far more (following therein the steps of the Church of Rome) than either the Scripture, the Articles of our Church, or the exposition of our Reverend Bishops and others, do. For the Fathers (say you) make the Sacraments only "*Seals*" of assurance, by which the Spirit worketh invisibly, to strengthen our faith: and therefore, they call them "visible words, seals of righteousness, and tokens of grace." That they do, and say thus, there is no man doubteth; but we are not yet persuaded that this is all, or "the furthest" (as you allege) "that they say; because undoubtedly we are assured, that they have learned both to know and to speak otherwise. For the Sacraments' "chiefest force, and virtue consisteth in this, That they are heavenly Ceremonies which God hath sanctified and ordained to be administered in his Church: First, as Marks to know when God doth impart his vital or Saving Grace of Christ, unto all that are capable thereof; and, secondly, as Means Conditional, which God requireth in them unto whom he imparteth Grace."§ For doubtless, it must needs be a great unthankfulness, and easily breed contempt, to ascribe only that power to them to be but as Seals; and that they teach but the mind, by other sense, as the Word doth by Hearing: which if it were all, what reason hath the Church to bestow any Sacrament upon Infants who as yet, for their years, are not capable of any instruction; "there is, therefore, of Sacraments, undoubtedly some more excellent and heavenly Use. Sacraments, by reason of their mixed nature, are more diversely interpreted, and disputed of than any other part of Religion besides; for that in so great store of

---

§ Jewel. Apol. Ang. cap. 10. div. 1.

properties belonging to the self-same thing, as every man's with hath taken hold of some especial consideration above the rest; so they have accordingly given their censure of the use and necessity of them. For if respect be had to the Duty which every communicant doth undertake, we may call them truly bonds of our obedience to God; strict obligations to the mutual exercise of Christian charity; provocations to godliness; preservations from sin; memorials of the principal benefits of Christ. If we respect the Time of their institution, they are annexed for ever unto the New Testament; as other Rites were before with the Old. If we regard the Weakness that is in us, they are warrants for the more security of our belief. If we compare the Receivers with those that receive them not, they are works§ of distinction to separate God's own from strangers; and in those that receive them as they ought, they are tokens of God's gracious presence, whereby men are taught, to know what they cannot see. For Christ and his Holy Spirit, with all their blessed effects, though entering into the soul of man we are not able to apprehend or express how, do notwithstanding give notice of the times when they use to make their access, because it pleaseth Almighty God to communicate, by sensible means, those blessings which are incomprehensible. Seeing, therefore, that Grace is a consequent of Sacraments; a thing which accompanieth them as their end; a benefit which he that hath, receiveth from God himself, the Author of Sacraments, and not from any other natural or supernatural quality in them; it may be hereby both understood, that Sacraments are necessary; and, that the manner of their necessity to life supernatural is not, in all respects, as food unto natural life. Because they contain in themselves, no vital force or efficacy; but they are duties of service and worship; which unless we perform as the Author of grace requireth, they are unprofitable: for, all receive not the grace of God, which receive the Sacraments of his grace. Neither is it, ordinarily, his will, to bestow the grace of Sacraments upon any, but by the Sacraments: which grace also, they that receive by Sacraments, or with Sacraments, receive it from him, and not

---

§ ["Marks," *sic* Hooker.

94

from them. That saving grace, which Christ originally is, or hath for the general good of his whole Church, by Sacraments he severally deriveth into every member thereof. They serve as Instruments; the use is in our hands, the effect is his." And this made the schoolmen, and the rest, (which you are afraid to grant) to say, that the sacraments were not only signs, but causes of our justification.† Now agent causes, we know, are of two sorts; principal, which worketh by the virtue and power of his [*its*] form; as, fire maketh hot: and thus, nothing can cause Grace, but God himself; Grace being a participation of "the Divine nature."‡ Instrumental, which worketh not as the other, by virtue of his [*its*] own proper form, but only by that motion which it hath from the principal, and first agent. Thus do Sacraments work; and therefore, saith St. Austin, the Sacraments are finished, performed, and pass away; but the virtue of God, that worketh by them, or with them, remaineth.§ Thus for the Use of them, the Church hath God's express commandment; for the Effect, his conditional promise; so that without our obedience to the one, there is of the other no apparent assurance; as contrariwise, where the Signs and Sacraments of his Grace are not, either through contempt unreceived, or received with contempt, we are not to doubt but that they really give what they promise, and are what they signify. For we take not the Sacraments (as it seemeth you do) for bare resemblances, or memorials of things absent; neither, for naked signs, and testimonies assuring us of Grace received before, but (as they are indeed and in truth) for means effectual, whereby God, when we take the Sacraments, delivereth into our hands that Grace, available unto eternal life; which Grace, the Sacraments represent or signify: and yet we acknowledge, as Hugo saith, that the Sacraments, being, as he calleth them, vessels of grace,‖ they cure not of themselves, no more than glasses do, the sick; but, the potions contained in them.¶ Neither doth any man say, (no, not the Church of Rome; although they be so accused, by some of us) that the Sacraments work of themselves, by a virtue resigned unto them, without God, merely of the work done actively; but that God worketh by

---

† Aquin. Part. III. quest. 62.   ‡ 2 Pet. i. 4.   § Cont. Faust. cap. 19.
‖ De Sacr. lib. i. cap. 4. † Bel. de Sacr. Tom. II. lib. ii. cap. 1. Calv. Inst. lib. iv. cap. 14. sect. 17.

them, as by instruments powerful, and thought in his wisdom fittest. For doubtless, the Church hath authority to use the Word and the Sacraments, as powerful means of regeneration, both having by a divine ordination, a force and virtue to beget Faith: and therefore justly, amongst all the treasures that God hath left unto his Church, we Honour and admire most, the holy Sacraments; not respecting so much the service which we do unto God in receiving them, as the dignity of that sacred and secret gift which we thereby receive from God. And therefore, when our Church saith, that "Sacraments are not only marks of Christian profession; but rather certain testimonies and effectual signs of Grace, and of the good-will of God towards us, by which God worketh invisibly in us;"* we thereby conceive, how Grace is indeed, the very end for which these heavenly mysteries were instituted; and, besides sundry other properties observed in them, the matter whereof they consist, is such as signifieth, figureth, and representeth their end: for surely Sacraments are the powerful instruments of God unto eternal life.† For, as the natural life consisteth in the union of the body with the soul; so the spiritual life, in the union of the soul with God. And forasmuch as there is no union of God with man, without that mean between both, which is both; nor this participated to us, without the Sacraments; the virtue must needs be great that God by these imparteth unto his Church. For they are Signs, not only signifying, but (as M. Zanchy saith) exhibiting‡ also invisible Grace. For God directly affirmeth, that he giveth that with the sign, which, by the sign he representeth. In the Sacraments, we acknowledge three things: The Word, the Element, the Thing signified by the Word and represented by the element; and all these united, yet not by any real or physical union, that one cannot be received without the other; but, in these, the union is sacramental, and the order mystical, betwixt the signs and the things signified, by an institution from God. Whereby it cometh to pass, the heavenly and spiritual things by signs bodily and earthly, are signified, offered, and by the virtue of the Holy Ghost, really exhibited, and

---

* Eccles. Ang. Art. XXV.   †"Alia sunt sacramenta dantia salutem, alia promittentia salvatorem." AUG. in Psalm lxxiii.   ‡ Exibentia. Zanch. in Decal. lib. i. cap. 16. p. 396.

performed unto the elect. Thus, if either the signs, or the thing signified, be wanting, it ceaseth truly to be a Sacrament. Neither is Grace necessarily tied ever to the external Sacrament: for we give the one, and God giveth the other; and, when both are given, then is the Sacrament faithfully received. Thus God justifieth "by the washing of the new birth, and the renewing of the Holy Ghost:"* for this being the effect of his promise, the Sacraments apply it unto us, by thus giving it; Faith by thus receiving; both, being as instruments. For God doth justify by the Sacraments; man, by Faith; but God, one and the same, maketh righteous by both; he being the author from whence they both come. Therefore "it is a branch of belief" (howsoever you scoff at it as omitted in our Creed), "That Sacraments are in their place," as Master Hooker saith, "no less required than belief itself. For when our Saviour promiseth eternal life, it is with this condition, as health to Naaman the Syrian,'Wash and be clean.'" But you are afraid to say that the Sacraments beget Faith, although you confess that they do increase it. Surely this is a fear like to the disposition of some melancholy humour where fancy, growing strong, forceth an avoidance of things oftentimes that are without danger: for to make Sacraments and the Word to be joined with Faith, both in his [its] generation, and in our justification, is neither to rob Faith of his [its] proper office, nor to ascribe more unto the Sacrament than of right belongeth. For we are not in any doubt to affirm, that the Sacraments, by the work done, actively, do not afford Grace; though rightly understood, passively, they may, by the work done: for in that justification and means of righteousness, whereof man is made partaker by the Sacraments, many things concur. First, in God's behalf, a Will that we should use those sensible elements; in Christ's behalf, his Passion, from which the Sacraments have their virtue; in the Minister's behalf, his Power, his Will; in the receiver's behalf, Will, Faith, Repentance; in respect of the Sacrament itself, the external action, which ariseth out of the fit application of the matter and the form of the Sacraments. Now, that which in all this, actively and instrumentally bringeth

---

* Tit. iii. 5.   † 2 Kings v. 14.

Grace, is the external action, which is commonly called the Sacrament: this having his [its] virtue from his [its] institution, and not from any merit, either in the Minister or in him that receiveth. For the Will of God, which useth the Sacraments as that means of Grace which it hath ordained, concurreth actively, but as a principal cause; the Passion of Christ concurreth as a cause meritorious; the Power and the Will of the Minister, necessarily concur, but as causes further removed; having their use only in effecting the sacramental action; in whose due circumstances, of administering, he is unwilling to fail. Will, Faith, and Repentance, are necessarily required in the Receiver that is of years; not as active causes, but as fit dispositions, for the subject; for Faith and Repentance, make not the sacramental grace, nor give power to the Sacrament; but only remove those lets, which are hindrances, that the Sacraments exercise not that virtue that is annexed to them. So that in Infants, in whom no such disposition is required, the Sacrament of Baptism is available without these. And therefore, to satisfy your demands in this Article, we conclude, That a man dying without Faith, and receiving the sacramental signs (for Sacraments he cannot receive) shall not be saved; and not receiving them (if his want be not either negligence or contempt) may be saved. Yet the latter to us is fearful, and ordinarily impossible; whereas the former is an evidence of our hope, and giveth most just reason charitably to judge. So that we say with St. Austin, "he that eateth and drinketh unworthily, eateth and drinketh his own damnation;* but he that contemneth to eat hath not life, and therefore shall not come to eternal life."† And yet those things that hurt the unworthy Receiver, do much profit him who receiveth them as he ought.

---

* 1 Cor. xi. 29. Cont. Faustum Manich. Tom. VI. lib. xiii. cap. 16. Cont. Epist. Parmen. lib. ii.
† "Dente non corde, foris non intus." AUG. "Habent ad testimonium damnationis, non ad adjutorium sanitatis." AUG. contra Liter. Petil. lib. ii. cap. 21.

ARTICLE XV.

OF CHRIST'S INSTITUTION.

It is not an apprehension equally incident unto the judgments of all wise men, rightly to conceive the true dependence of things. For those who allow and confess actions to have much virtue, oftentimes do mistake from whence that virtue cometh: this; as it happeneth in causes of more usual and known nature, so it is sometimes even in those things where the author is but one, and he incomparably the best; because he vouchsafeth to admit instruments of a lower condition, to be agents in the performance of things of so great an use. This maketh men, in the Sacraments —those holy institutions of God left unto the Church—often to fail, in a due estimation of them. And, when they do grant their use to be singular; yet even then, to doubt whereupon this dependeth: because the same things, performed by divers, are not the same; and those which admit no difference in respect of substance, yet are subject, in regard of some circumstance, to an alteration, either more or less. From hence, hath proceeded the difference in this article, which, over violently, you urge to be betwixt Master Hooker and our Church; of whom (as usually you do), you carry too jealous a suspicion of too great agreement with the Church of Rome. That Sacraments have a virtue, even more than to be only Signs, is already proved: but, whether this virtue be less where the Minister hath moe [*more*] faults, or none at all, where his intention is not to administer a Sacrament; that cometh now to be discussed in this place. To make the Sacraments depend, for their grace, upon the Integrity of men, were to deny the benefit to a great number without cause; and to punish men for a fault that were none of theirs. The first of these is denied by few; nay, some are so far from opinion, that Sin in the Minister is any let to the Sacrament, that they are not afraid to affirm that Sacraments are effectual, though administered by Satan himself.* Doubtless few (saving only some Anabaptists) deny the efficacy of the Sacraments, for the defects of life in the lawful dispensers of them. They are inestimable favours unto God's Church, not to be measured by the hand from whom immediately we receive them, but by that Almighty Power, the fountain of all goodness, from whence they do first come. For as amongst men it were want either of judgment or civility, or both, less to esteem of the benefit for the meanness of the messenger, where we are undoubtedly assured that it is the Prince's seal; so in the Sacraments, we must esteem them as the seals and favours of God himself, whatsoever the imperfections are, in those Ministers from whom we have them. For the defects of men, being in the Church and Lawfully called to those Functions, no way touch the efficacy of the Sacraments, whose virtue dependeth upon a higher power. And therefore, we deny all reiteration of Baptism, whatsoever the defects, for manners, are in those that do first give it. For we are equally baptized into the "name of the Father, the Son, and the Holy Ghost," what unworthiness, or inequality soever, remain in the persons that do baptize. For the holiness of the Sacraments is in no way polluted by the uncleanness of the hands that give them. For those Sacraments which unreverently being handled, as St. Austin saith, do hurt the giver, yet, even by their hands, profit those that receive them worthily.† It was, both in Asia and Africa, an error long since, That the Sacraments were not firm, which were administered by Heretics, or Schismatics separated from the unity of the Church.‡ The first author of this, was Agrippinus Bishop of Carthage, whom St. Cyprian succeeded, as St. Austin writeth; and was a little infected with the same error.§ After these, were the Donatists: but we will not labour for confirmation of this point, because you object

---

* Luth. de Missa privat. Edit. anno 1534.
* Aug. cont. Donatist. lib. iv. cap. 13. Cont. Epist. Parm. lib. ii. cap. 10.
† Euseb. Hist. lib. vii. cap. 6. et cap. 2.   ‡ De Baptis. lib. ii.

nothing against Master Hooker in it. And it is no controversy at all betwixt us and the Church of Rome; and therefore, we say with the ancient Fathers, Stephanus, Siricius, Innocentius the First, Leo, Anastasius the Second in his epistle to Anastasius the Emperor;‖ with the Councils; first the General Council of Nice, often alleged by St. Austin to this end;* the first Council of Carthage,† the last assembly at Trent; with the testimonies of Fathers and Doctors; and, according to the Articles of our Church by you alleged, That "by the malice of wicked men which are over the administration of the Sacraments, the effect of the things ordained by Christ is not taken away, or the grace of God's gifts diminished, as touching them which receive by Faith and orderly the things offered unto them; which for the institution of Christ, and his promise, are effectual, although they be administered by evil men." But, to infer hereupon, that the same actions, howsoever done, scoffingly and in jest, contrary or besides the holy institution of the Church, are truly Sacraments; it is a conclusion too violent, and not warranted by any truth. For howsoever the grace of Sacraments dependeth not upon the Minister, who may fail of these virtues that are fit to be required in him; yet it is necessary, that there should be an Intention to administer a true Sacrament, lest we put no difference betwixt that which either derision, imitation, chance, or the Church doth. For, if the conversion of Lucius first Christian king of this Land were to be acted upon a Stage, and that two persons were to represent Fugatius and Damianus, set by Eleutherius the Pope to baptize Lucius,§ could any man in reason think, how orderly soever performed, that this were true baptism? Were not this, to make the bare action, all, and the Intention a circumstance not belonging to it? But we must know, as Mr Hooker saith, that "Sacraments are actions, mystical and religious (for no man can truly define them otherwise), which nature they have not, unless they proceed from a serious meaning: yet what every man's private mind is, as we cannot know, so neither are we bound to examine; for

---

‖ Euseb. lib. vii. cap. 2. in. epist. i. ad Himerium. Epist. xxii. ad Maced. Episc. Epist. lxxvii. ad Nicetam.　　* De Bapt. lib. ii. cap. 3-7, 9.　　† Circa Ann. 327
§Circa Ann. 165.

in these cases, the known intent of the Church, doth generally suffice; and where the contrary is not manifest (as circumstances will serve easily to discover), we must presume that he which outwardly doth the work, hath inwardly the purpose of the Church of God."‖ Now, this being a discreet rule, Wisely to put a difference betwixt Sacraments (holy actions) and the like irreligiously and profanely performed; is that whereat your zealous wisdom doth take offence, and which you pursue with that bitterness of speech, (calling it "mere Popery, a human invention, and inducement to Fides implicita") as though the dangers were neither few, nor small, which came unto the Church by this opinion. Let me entreat your patience a little, and vouchsafe to be but advised by him who, in all humility, will be ready to follow the sound directions of the meanest in God's Church; and I doubt not, to make it apparent that Master Hooker hath delivered that truth, the contrary whereof is no way fit to be admitted or allowed by us. Some are of opinion, that no Intention at all is required in the Ministers of the Sacraments, but that if the Thing and the Words be present, though either in jest or otherwise performed, yet notwithstanding it is a Sacrament.* The first Author of this, as Bellarmine saith,§ was Luther, whose words I must needs say, are violently wrested, to make him speak that which he never meant.‡ It is like that he, out of whom, by misunderstanding, you have collected this opinion, was Master Calvin; who, rightly deriving the virtue of Sacraments from the Minister to God himself, the author of the first institution, saith thus; "I refer, so much to the holy institution of Christ, that if an Epicure, inwardly deriding the whole action, should administer the Supper, by the commandment of Christ" (mark the words) "and according to the Rule by him given, (which no man could that wanted the Intention of the Church) I would account them," saith he, "the true pledges of the body and the blood of Christ:"§ Where we are willing to confess with him, and with truth itself, That Sacraments for their virtue, depend not upon the Intention of the Minister

---

* But—Sacramentum est Sacra actio.
† De Sacra. lib. i. cap. 27.   ‡ Lib. de Missa privata.
§ In Audit. Concilii. Trid. sess. 7. can. 2.   ‖ *Ubi sup*

though without the Intention of the Church they are not Sacraments. Where, by Intention, we mean not a particular purpose, of all that the Sacraments require (a thing peradventure above the capacity of many Lawful Ministers), but a general Intention, of performing that sacred action according to the meaning of the Church. Where, by Church, we mean not any one particular, but the true Church; or as Mr. Calvin saith, Christ's "Rule," or that Intention which Christians in that action have; and yet, if one in this should follow the Intention of a particular Church that did err, it were not a reason sufficient to make the Sacrament to be none at all: for even his Intention, in following that particular Church though erring, were an Intention of following the True Church, that doth not err. Neither is it required, as the Schoolmen say, That this Intention necessarily be actual; nor it sufficeth not, to be habitual, (which may be in men either drunk or asleep) but virtual, that is, in the power of that Intention which howsoever now distracted, before was actual.‖ Neither do we mean, that the Minister should necessarily have the same intent of the end, which the Church hath, but of the action; the end being, perhaps, without the compass of his knowledge, but the action cannot; unless we suppose him to be a Minister weaker than any Church hath. For it is one thing, to intend what the Church intendeth; and another thing, to intend what the Church doth: for those that intend by Baptism, an utter acquittance from original sin, and those that do not, there is a diversity in the end, but the action is all one; and therefore not reiterated, though the end be diverse. Now, to do the external action, and yet in jest, is no more to do what the Church intendeth to do, than their speech and action, "Hail, King of the Jews,"* was any honour, or true reverence, to our Saviour Christ. The necessity of this Intention (not for grace, but to make it a Sacramental action), will more evidently appear, if we consider what kind of Instrument the Minister is. Man may be the instrument of another agent, many ways. First, in respect only of his bodily members; his hand, his back, or such like; without any use of the will. Secondly, in respect of his outward

---

* [Matt. xxvii. 29.]   ‖Tho. Aquin. part. 3. quest. 64. art. 8.

parts, with the use of sense; as to read, to watch, to tell what he seeth; and to this also, the will is no further required, but to the outward action. Thirdly, in respect of the bodily members, together with sense and reason; as in Judges appointed by Princes to determine causes, wherein wisdom and the will are to be instruments. Now the Ministers of the Sacrament must be of this third kind. And therefore, saith Hugo, "if a father should take his son to a bath, and should say, 'Son, I wash thee in the name of the Father, and of the Son, and of the Holy Ghost,' and so dip him in the water, it were ridiculous to think that he were thus baptized."† Where, although such profaners are without excuse, for unreverend imitation of holy things, yet these actions, without the Intention of the Church, can no ways be termed Sacraments. For, if those who hold a sermon read, to be no sermon, and yet a prayer read, to be a prayer, require "that the Spirit of grace and prayer be not wanting in the party reading, and the hearers;"‡ how can we think those actions to be Sacramental, where, in the Minister, there is not so much as an Intention that they should be Sacraments? And therefore, saith Hugo, in the place before alleged, "Alexander the Bishop held the Baptism that Athanasius ministered to other boys in play,§ to be true Baptism, because he did it with an Intention of true Baptism." In those that are but instruments (as the Minister is no more), the virtues of faith, hope, and charity, are not requisite; and yet because they are reasonable instruments, their actions must proceed from election, and Intention. Therefore, we conclude, That this Intention of the Church, is no ground of uncertainty, seeing she 'tendeth but one thing; that is, to perform them as Sacraments; nor giveth any power to the virtue of the Sacrament; and that the Church cannot make a Sacrament; but, to distinguish betwixt actions religious, and the same not religious, there is required the Intention of the Church.

---

* De Sacra. lib. ii. part. 6. cap. 13. † Perk. upon the Lord's Prayer p. 143. Impr. 1596.
§ Ruff. lib. x. cap. 14. Sozem. lib. ii. cap. 16. Niceph. lib. viii. cap. 40.

ARTICLE XVI.

OF THE NECESSITY OF BAPTISM

Where many things are doubted of without reason, it is neither easy, nor usually expedient, to answer all. Wisdom esteemeth it much fitter to pass by, without yielding satisfaction to some apparent truths called in question, rather than by answering, to let the simple understand that men have doubted of those points. For, the first calling in question of unfallible truths, gave strength to evil minds to find out all shews of reason for maintaining of those things which their own weakness, at first, made them simply to mistake. So that, whosoever maketh every doubt to be a contention; or, laboureth to confute errors of long continuance; in the first, kindleth but that spark which, without some breath, would easily die; and in the later, must arm himself to encounter an obstinate resolution. The consideration of this, made me not willing, either to dispute the new born doubts of your own, in this Article; which being discussed, in time, might grow to be old errors; or, to bestow labour, for the assisting of that truth which, out of great judgment and learning, hath often been defended by other men's pains. But, seeing it is an usual false conclusion, as, to argue a lawfulness from what we do, so, a want of ability from what we do not; I thought it fitter, even following their steps that have gone before me, rather to resolve others what you have doubted of in this point, than that any should conclude, out of silence, an impossibility that you could be answered. For the willingness that some men have to do more than they are able, maketh others suspected to want ability, in whom there appeareth not the same willingness. If all men rightly considered, in those actions that concern man's Salvation, how far we are tied not only in obedience, but for use, to those things that are means to effect the same; few would have been so carelessly resolute, to contemn Good Works, through an opinion of an eternal election; or, so negligently have despised the only door of entrance into the Church (Baptism) through an opinion that God doth save, even where this is wanting. We do all confess, That Baptism is a Sacrament of regeneration, or new birth, by water in the Word of life; that it is a sign, nay, a means of initiation, whereby we are cooped into the society of the Church:* Thus, by this being ingrafted into Christ, we may be taken for the sons of God; and so receive new names to be called Christians: And therefore learned men have thought it "to be the door of our actual entrance into God's house; the first apparent being of life," as St. Basil calleth it; "the first step of our sanctification," as Master Hooker saith.* "For as we are not naturally men, without birth, so neither are we Christian men in the eye of the Church, without new birth;" we say, in the eye of the Church, for we take not upon us, to see as God doth, who knoweth without all means, both to make, and, without visible tokens, is able to discern, who belong unto him: and yet, in our eye, Baptism is that "which both declareth and maketh us to be Christians." Therefore, it is a strange opinion of them, who say, that "he which is not a Christian before Baptism, cannot be made a Christian by Baptism; which is only the seal of the grace of God, before received."§ These, as it seemeth you do, elevate too much the ordinary and immediate means of life; relying wholly upon the bare conceit of that eternal election, which notwithstanding, includeth a subordination of means; without which, we are not actually brought to enjoy what God secretly did intend. And therefore, to build upon God's election, if we keep not ourselves to the ways which he hath appointed for men to walk in, is but a self-deceiving vanity: for all men, notwithstanding their preordination unto life (which none can know but God only) are in the Apostle's

---

* Roman Catecis.　　　† Cal. Inst. lib. iv. [cap. 15. sect. 6.]　　§ T.C. lib. iii. p. 134

opinion, till they have embraced the truth, but "the children of wrath, as well as others."‖ And, howsoever "the children of the Faithful, are born holy," as you allege out of that reverend Bishop,¶ and the Elect, are adopted to be the sons of God in their predestination, yet afterwards when they believe, then they are said more properly to be the sons of God indeed: for although it be true as St. Paul saith, that your sons are "holy,"* namely, when they are born, by reason of the promise; yet he saith, that we are sanctified by faith, meaning actually and indeed. For as kings (in those kingdoms that are by election) are first chosen, then designed, then crowned, which last action is that which maketh them full, and complete kings; so whatsoever we were, in that secret election to us unknown, yet then, when we are baptized, † and not before, we are properly, publicly, solemnly joined unto God, and admitted into his Church.‡Yet we exclude not (neither doth any that I know) these benefits thus bestowed, ordinarily, in and with Baptism; but that extraordinarily (sometimes before, as in Paul and Cornelius; sometimes after, as in many baptized by heretics; sometimes without, as in those who prevent their baptism by martyrdom, and some others;) these benefits may be bestowed. For, it were a "fearful doctrine, injurious to many thousand souls, and blasphemous against the bottomless mercy of a most loving Father," to exclude all those from eternal life, whom not negligence or contempt, but some other occasion, hath hindered to be baptized. And, therefore, it is strange, that you would make Mr. Hooker to speak for so absolute a necessity (which indeed he doth not) but maketh it limited; or that yourself would dislike a necessity, whereas you confess,this to be the "condition of Baptism, if it cannot be had as it ought"** The matter then principally called in question in this Article, is What kind of Necessity there is of baptism; a thing already fully handled by Mr. Hooker;‡ and therefore we will be more sparing in this point. All things, which

---

‖ Ephes. ii. 3.   ¶ Jewel, in the Def. of Apol. par. 2. p. 150.   * 1 Cor. vii. 14.
† 1 Cor. xii. 13.   ‖‖ Zanch. in Decal. p. 400.
§ "Non enim ista tribuunt quod per ista tribuitur." HUGO. lib. *de Sacra.* cap. 3.

108

either procured, or men delivered from grievous evil, the same we must needs
confess Necessary: now we know, there is necessary absolute, and there is a
necessity conditional, and even that conditional , for the end in ordinary estimation,
is absolutely necessary. are known causes, or fit means, whereby any great good is
usually either procured, or men delivered from grievous evil, the same we must needs
confess Necessary: now we know, there is a necessity absolute, and there is a
necessity conditional, and even that conditional, for the end in ordinary estimation,
is absolutely necessary. Thus, to a man in the sea to escape drowning, we account
a ship a necessary means, even of absolute necessity in respect of our judgment,
howsoever some few have escaped by other means; so our Saviour saith of Baptism,
"unless a man be born again of water and of the Holy Ghost, he cannot enter into the
kingdom of heaven." Which place we understand, howsoever some deny it, of
Baptism, by material water, according to the general consent of the ancient Fathers:
For it is a rule in expounding the Scriptures, that where a literal construction will
stand (as in this place), the farthest from the letter is commonly the worst. And
therefore, water and the Spirit both concurring in that Sacrament, why should there
not be, though not an equal, yet, a necessity of both? For, as the Spirit is necessary
to regeneration, so regeneration is necessary to eternal life; which so far dependeth
upon the outward Sacrament, that God will have it embraced not only as sign or
token what we receive, as you affirm, but also as an instrument, or mean, whereby
we receive it; and this without any enthralling, as you seem to fear, of God's merciful
grace. Neither, as Hugo saith, do these give (speaking of the Sacraments) that which
is given by these, and yet ordinarily as necessary to receive these,§ as those graces
are necessary which we receive by these. For, though Baptism be not a cause of
Grace, yet the grace which is given by Baptism, doth so far depend upon the very
outward Sacrament, as God will have it embraced as a necessary means whereby we
receive the same: and howsoever we dare not judge those that in some cases do want

§ John iii.5.

it, yet we may boldly gather, that he whose mercy now vouchsafeth to bestow the means, hath also, long since, intended us that whereunto they lead. For to imagine, nothing Necessary, but Faith, is to come near the error of the old Valentinian heretics, who ascribed all to Knowledge only.* So saith Tertullian.† Some account the Sacraments, as, unprofitable, without Faith, so, needless, where Faith is; but no Faith can be profitable , saith St. Bernard, to him, who when he may, yet refuseth to receive the Sacraments.‡ Therefore, if Christ himself which giveth salvation, require Baptism, it is not for us to dispute or examine, Whether those that are unbaptized, may be saved; but, seriously to do that which is required, and religiously to fear the danger which may grow by the want thereof. For doubtless, the Sacrament of Baptism, in respect of God the author of the institution, may admit dispensation; but in respect of us, who are tied to obey, there is an absolute necessity. For it is in the power of God without these to save; but it is not in the power of man, without these to come to salvation.§ And yet the Church holdeth constantly, as well touching other believers, as Martyrs, That Baptism taken away by necessity, taketh not away the necessity of Baptism; but is supplied by the desire thereof. For "what is there in us," saith St. Ambrose, "more than to will and to seek for our own good? Thy servant Valentinian (who died before he was baptized) O Lord, did both." For as the visible sign, may be without true holiness, so the invisible sanctification, saith St. Austin, may sometimes be without the visible sign. And yet these are no just reasons, either to make us presume, or to take away the necessity of this holy sacrament:¶ for even those have it in their wish, as the Schoolmen say, who indeed do want the same.** And howsoever, as they of Rhemes confess, "such may be the grace of God towards men, that they may have remission, justification and sanctification before the external sacrament of Baptism; as, in Peter's preaching they all received the Holy Ghost before the Sacrament; yet this is no ordinary thing now in Infants, and, whosoever

---

* Iren. Con. Her. lib. i. cap. 18. † De Baptism. ‡ Epist. 70. ad Hugo.
§ Hug. de Sacra. lib. i. cap. 5. ¶ Quest. Vet. Test. lib. iii. cap. 84.
** Aqui. part. 3. quest. 68. art. 2. *voto, nonre.*

110

therefore shall contemn them, cannot be saved.‡‡ Yet "God, who hath not bound his grace, in respect of his own freedom, to any Sacrament, may and doth accept them as baptized which either are martyred before they could be baptized, or else depart this life with wish and desire to have that Sacrament, which by some remediless necessity they could not obtain."‡ For "the just, by what death soever he be prevented, his soul shall be in rest."§ And, whereas you demand, Whether our Sacraments be not the same in nature, virtue, and substance, that the Sacraments of the Jews were under the Law;" and therefore, Baptism to be of no more necessity, than circumcision; we answer with St. Austin, "The Sacraments delivered by Christ, are for number, fewer (taking, as Master Zanchy noteth, Sacraments largely for all those ceremonies as he did); for performance, easier; for understanding, more excellent; for observation, more chaste. And therefore, though all Sacraments for their substance be one (that is Christ), and that more particularly Baptism succeedeth Circumcision: yet their difference is great, both in their rites which were divers, and in the manner of the object; the one Christ to come, the other already come;* the one a corporal benefit, to be of that Church which should have her certain seat until the coming of the Messias, in the land of Canaan; the other expecting a spiritual kingdom. The one, bound to an observation of the whole Law, Ceremonial, Judicial, Moral; the other, only to the Moral Law; and for want of true fulfilling of it, to faith and repentance. The one, to Israel only; the other, to the whole Church. The one, to continue till the coming of the Messias in humility; the other, until his coming in glory. The one belonged unto the males only, the other to all."† So that as the differences were many, and not small: even so we doubt not to affirm, that the benefits are far more; and the necessity is much greater. And therefore, as Master Hooker saith, "We have for Baptism no day set, as the Jews had for Circumcision; neither have we by the Law of God, but only by the Church's discretion, a place

†† In Act. Apost. x. 47.   ‡Test. in Job. iii. 5.   § Wisd. iv. 7.
§ "Petra erat Christus." 1 Cor. x. 4. Coloss. ii. 11–13.   † De Doctrin. Christ. lib. iii. cap. 3.

thereunto appointed. Baptism therefore even in the meaning of the Law of Christ, belongeth unto infants capable thereof, from the very instant of their birth; which if they have not howsoever, rather than lose it by being put off, because some circumstances of solemnity do not concur, the Church, as much as in her lieth" (mark the words, for she cannot disappoint God's eternal election) but as far as in her power, by denying the means, "casteth away their souls:" and therefore there is a more absolute Necessity, in the Church to give Baptism, which she can never willingly refuse to do without cruelty, than there is in the Faithful to receive it, who, how willing soever, yet always cannot.

CHAPTER XVII.

OF TRANSUBSTATIATION

Seeing the Church hath nothing left unto it, either more powerful or more reverently to be esteemed, than the holy Sacraments; it hath been the policy of Satan, from the beginning, to darken the clear light of these, with infinite clouds of unnecessary questions, wholly impertinent and unprofitable to that cause. So that out of due consideration of this great evil, wise men have thought it more fit, by application, to make use of that which concerns them, in this kind, rather than, by curious inquisition, to desire to find out what concerneth them not.. The whole benefit which the Church hath, is from Christ; and this, by no other means but by participation: For, Christ to be what he is, is not to be what he is to the Church, but only by a participation of all that he is (as a Mediator) betwixt him and us. This we call the mutual, inward hold, which Christ hath of us and we of him; in such sort, that each possesseth other, by way of special interest, properly, and inherent copulation: for what soever we are eternally, according to his election, we are actually no longer in God, than only from the time of our actual adoption into the body of his true Church; into the fellowship of his children:* we are therefore adopted sons of God to eternal life by participation of the only Son of God, whose life is the well-spring and cause of ours.† This participation, besides the presence of Christ's person, and besides the mystical copulation thereof with the parts and members of his whole Church, importeth a true, actual, influence of grace, whereby the life which we live according to godliness, is his,‡ and from him we receive those perfections wherein

---

*Col ii. 10   † John xiv. 19.   ‡ Gal. ii. 20.

our eternal happiness consisteth. This is partly, by imputation of his merit; partly, by habitual and real infusion of his grace; the first whereof, as the ground of all the rest, being the Spirit, maketh a blessed union of all those,-howsoever distinguished by place, or time,-who mystically belong unto that body; and this, being the common union of all Saints, we fitly term, the Communion of Saints. That of imputation, maketh us all sons; in which number, how far soever one may seem to excel another; yet, touching this, that all are sons, they are all equals; some happily better sons than the rest are, but none any more a son than another. Neither doth this participation include any gross surmise of any mixture of the substance of his flesh with outs; but is actually derived unto his Church by the use of his holy Sacraments: wherein Baptism doth challenge unto itself the inchoation of those graces, the consummation whereof dependeth upon other mysteries. For the grace which we have by the holy Eucharist doth not begin, but continue life; and therefore, no man receiveth it before Baptism, because nothing is capable of nourishment that doth not live. Now, life being propounded to all men as their end; those which, by Baptism, have laid the foundation, and attained the first beginning of a new life, have, in the Eucharist, food prescribed and given for the continuance of life in them. In both, the same thing being afforded (which is a participation of Christ), "in our infancy we are incorporated into Christ, and, by Baptism, receive the grace of his Spirit without any sense of feeling of the gift which God bestoweth; in the Eucharist, we so receive the gift of God, that we know by grace what the grace is which God giveth us; the degrees of our increase in holiness and virtue we see, and can judge of them; we understand, that the strength of our life begun in Christ, is Christ; that his flesh is meat, and his blood drink, not by surmised imagination, but truly, even so truly, that through Faith, we perceive in the body and blood sacramentally presented, the very taste of eternal life; the grace of the Sacrament is here as the food which we eat and drink." And howsoever it was to be feared, that by the means of some, men should be brought to account of this Sacrament but only as of a shadow, destitute, empty, and void of Christ: yet, now at length, for any thing that I can see, all sides are grown, as it is fit, to a general agreement concerning that which alone is material, namely, the real participation of Christ, and of life, in his body and blood, by means of this Sacrament. The manner how, which ought to be the least part of our consideration, is, in this question, the greatest difference. So that, considering the small success that bitter contentions have had in this cause, it were to be wished, "that men would give themselves more to meditate with silence what they have by the Sacrament; and, in humility, less to dispute of the manner how." This being the true difference betwixt Christ's disciples, and other, That "the one, because they enjoyed not, disputed; the other, disputed not because they enjoyed." For, doubtless, this heavenly food is given for the satisfying of our empty souls, and not for the exercising of our curious and subtle wits. It is sufficient, that the Sacraments really exhibit what they promise; though they are not really, or do not really contain in themselves, that Grace, which with them, or by them, it pleaseth God to bestow. Now the first, by all sides being granted, "why do we vainly," (saith Master Hooker), "trouble ourselves with so fierce contentions, whether by Consubstantiation, or else by Transubstantiation, the Sacrament itself be first possessed with Christ or no? A thing which no way can either further of hinder us, howsoever it stand, because our participation of Christ in the sacrament dependeth upon the co-operation of his omnipotent power which maketh it his body and blood to us, whether with change or without alteration of the element, such as they imagine, we need not greatly to care or inquire for: That being admitted, wherein all agree (which is a real presence), why should not the rest in question, rather be left as superfluous than urged as necessary." This is that which being uttered by Master Hooker out of great wisdom, argueth as your surmise, that he maketh "light of the doctrine of Transubstantiation; whereas the reverend Fathers of our Church do so much detest it; and that so may blessed Martyrs, have suffered death for denial thereof! Whether the doctrine of Transubstantiation be true or false (howsoever it is plain what Master Hooke thought) yet, that is no par to the contention as this time. The matter in question betwixt you and him, is only this, Whether it be not curiosity, to

116

contend for the matter how, seeing all sides are agreed, that the thing is? For, as in those who were to be cured by our Saviour Christ, we ought not curiously to inquire how the hem of his garment had such virtue, but faithfully to believe that it was able to afford health; so, neither in this, need the Church to be inquisitive after what manner Christ presenteth himself, but truly to believe that he is there present. Which, because some irreligious men, at the first, doubted; men have been driven to find out these reasonable satisfactions, or rather, satisfactions to human reason, from his Omnipotency, Transubstantiation, Consubstantiation, or such like; whereas, indeed, we know, that in many mysteries of our Faith, it is sufficient to believe the thing, though we cannot comprehend the means, how. Of this kind, saith Bellarmine, is the Trinity of persons in the Unity of essence: Christ to be both God, and man; the same bodies in number to rise again; Christ really to be in the Eucharist; and such like, which by reason of our shallow understanding, man's weakness is not able to comprehend.† For, if ignorance be in these things that are below,‡ then how much more in those things that are above! And if Mephibosheth, when he came unto David's table, accounted himself in all humility, so far unworthy;§ what ought our contemplation to be, but of His mercy, and our want of desert, when we shall come to be partakers of so inestimable favours? For if the Bethshemites were punished for looking into the Ark,‖ what can we expect to be the recompense of our indiscreet folly? Is it not, then, an advice needful, which Master Hooker giveth, and you mislike, rather to seek how to receive it worthily, than to desire to know how it is present with us? For the one importeth a duty that is necessary, and the other bewrayeth a desire, that is superfluous, in the one we perform what God hath commanded, and in the other, affect, what he hath forbidden. Neither is this to make Transubstantiation (for denial whereof so many, as you say, have died) any light matter, but rather to shew the great depth of the mystery, and the small profit that is reaped by the searching of it: for seeing "it is on all sides plainly confest, First, that

---

† De Sacra. lib. ii. cap. 1   ‡ Eccles. viii. 17.   § 2 Sam. ix. 8.   ‖ 1 Sam. vi. 19.

this Sacrament is a true and real participation of Christ, who thereby imparteth himself, even his whole entire person, as a mystical head, unto every soul that receiveth him, and that every such receiver doth thereby incorporate or unite himself unto Christ as a mystical member of him, yea of them also, whom he acknowledgeth to be his own. Secondly, that to whom the person of Christ is thus communicated, to them he giveth, by the same Sacrament, his Holy Spirit to sanctify them, as it sanctifieth him which is their Head. Thirdly, that what merit, force, or virtue soever, there is in this sacrificed body and blood, we freely, fully, and wholly have it by this Sacrament. Fourthly, that the effect thereof in us, is a real transmutation of our souls and bodies from sin to righteousness, from death and corruption to immortality and life. Fifthly, that because the Sacrament, being of itself but a corruptible and earthly creature, must needs be thought an unlikely instrument to work so admirable effects in man, we are therefore to rest ourselves altogether upon the strength of his glorious power who is able and will bring to pass, that the bread and cup, which he giveth us shall be truly the thing he promiseth." Now seeing there are but three differing opinions for the manner of it; Sacramentaries, Transubstantiation, and Consubstantiation; and all so plead God's Omnipotency; the first, "to that alteration which the rest confess he accomplisheth; the patrons of transubstantiation, over and besides that, to the change of one substance into another; the followers of consubstantiation, to the kneading up of both substances, as it were, in one lump;" and that, in this variety "The mind which loveth truth, and seeketh comfort out of holy mysteries, hath not perhaps the leisure, perhaps not the wit nor capacity to tread out so endless mazes as the intricate disputes of this cause have led men into, how should a virtuously disposed mind better resolve with itself than thus? "Variety of judgments, and opinions argueth obscurity in those things whereabout they differ; but that which all parts receive for certain, that which every one having sifted, is by one denied or doubted of, must needs be matter of infallible truth: whereas therefore there are but three expositions made of, This is my body; the first, This is in itself before participation really and truly the natural substance of my body, by reason of the co-existence which my omnipotent body hath with the sanctified element of bread;-which is the Lutheran's interpretation: The second, This is in itself and before participation the very true and natural substance of my body by force of that Deity, which by the words of consecration abolisheth the substance of bread, and substituteth in the place thereof my body;-which is the construction of the Church of Rome: The last, This hallowed food, through concurrence of divine power, is, in verity and truth, unto faithful receivers, instrumentally a cause of that mystical participation, whereby, as I make myself wholly theirs, so I give them in hand an actual possession of all such saving grace as my sacrificed body can yield, and all their souls so presently need; this is to them, and in them, by body.-Of these three rehearsed interpretations, the last hath in it nothing but what the rest do all approve and acknowledge to be most true; nothing but that which the words of Christ are, on all sides confest to enforce; nothing but that which the Church of God hath always thought necessary; nothing but that which alone is sufficient for every Christian man to believe concerning the use and force of this sacrament; finally, nothing but that wherewith the writings of all antiquity are consonant, and all Christian confessions agreeable. And as truth, in what kind soever, is by no kind of truth gainsaid; so the mind, which resteth itself on this, is never troubled with those perplexities which the other do both find, by means of so great contradiction between their opinions and the true principles of reason grounded upon experience, nature and sense. What moveth us to argue how life should be bread, our duty being but to take what is offered, and most assuredly to rest persuaded of this, that if we can but eat we are safe? "Such as love piety will, as much as in them lieth, know all things that God commandeth, but especially the duties of service which they owe unto him: as for his dark and hidden works, they prefer (as becometh them in such cases) simplicity of faith before that knowledge, which curiously sifting what it should adore, and disputing too boldly of that which the wit of man cannot search, chilleth, for the most part, all warmth of zeal, and bringeth soundness of belief, many times, into great hazard. Let it therefore be sufficient for me, presenting myself at the Lord's Table, to know what there I receive from him, without searching or inquiring of the manner how Christ performeth his promise; let disputes and questions,—enemies to piety, abatements of true devotion, and hitherto in this case but over patiently heard,—let them take their rest; let curious and sharp-witted men beat their heads about what questions themselves will; the very letter of the word of Christ giveth plain security, that these mysteries do, as nails, fasten us to his cross, that by them we draw out (as touching efficacy, force, and virtue) even the blood of his wounded side; that this bread hath more in it, than our eyes behold; that this cup hallowed with solemn benediction, availeth to the endless life and welfare both of soul and body, in that it serveth as well for a medicine to heal our infirmities and purge our sins, as for a sacrifice of thanksgiving; which [*with*] touching it santifieth; it enlighteneth with belief; it truly conformeth us unto the Image of Jesus Christ. What these elements are in themselves it skilleth not; it is enough, that to me which take them they are the body and blood of Jesus Christ; his promise in witness hereof sufficeth; his word he knoweth which way to accomplish; why should any cogitation possess the mind of a faithful communicant but this, "O my God, thou ar true! O my soul, thou are happy!" to dehort, then, from violence of disputing, and curiosity of seeking in a matter needless to know, being (as Master Calvin saith) incomprehensible what fault can you find, in Master Hooker? Doth he not dissuade from this, in zeal, only to draw to a better contemplation? Can this in reason be termed any "gentle construction of Popish opinions, or privily to rob the truth of our English Creed of her due estimation?" Think not so uncharitably of one whose principal care was, in the midst of all his knowledge, only to follow that Truth, soundly and uncorruptly, which was available and sufficient to save himself. Many itch with curiosity; they are not few, that do blow contentions, to make them kindle; some desire to know, only that they may know; some others, that they may be known; he doubtless, with humble sobriety both in this and in all other points, to comprehend that which was most available for the true direction of others, and the salvation of his own soul. And therefore, to you objections in this article, which are neither great nor many, I have framed my answer, most out of his mouth who fullest understood this cause, and ought to be esteemed the best interpreter of his own meaning.

ARTICLE XVIII.

OF SPECULATIVE DOCTRINE.

As wise Physicians, in the curing of some diseases, neglect not that habit of the body which, when the disease is cured, may threaten a relapse; because evils past leave a disposition for the like to come; and, by returning, are so much the more dangerous, by how much the strength of the sick is less able to make resistance; –so fareth it with us, in the labour employed about these articles that follow: wherein if you had well considered, the serious superscription of your Letter, that it was for "resolution in matters of doctrine," and those of no small moment, but such as "seem" (it is well you said *seem*) "to overthrow the foundation of Christian religion, and of the Church amongst us," these articles that follow, might very fitly have been omitted by you. For, though all that you object be far from that mature judgment, which ought to be in such as you desire to seem; yet these, concerning Speculative Doctrine, the naming of Master Calvin, Schoolmen, or Master Hooker's style, how can they be called matters of Doctrine, or in any construction be thought to weaken "the foundation of the Church amongst us?" But seeing, in the former, we have done somewhat to cure that distemper (the effect of too much choler) which, being suffered to increase, might grow dangerous; it is not amiss, gently to apply something, even to these, which wanting the malice of any dangerous disease, yet are infallible tokens of a distempered habit. Neither need we in this, to make any other defence for the right use of those sentences which you reprehend, saving only to set down to the reader's eye, the sentence at large, which you have maimed by severing; and challenging him, in those things which are incomparably excellent, you have

122

manifestly discovered your weakness of understanding. But, as in any curious workmanship where the parts are not disjointed, there appeareth the admirable effects of a skilful hand, which rudely being severed, and rashly pulled in pieces, blemish the beauty of the former work, and make many things seem, in the eye of ignorance, to be idle and of no use; so fareth it with those speeches which, in this Article, so unseasonably are distasted by you, which if any indifferent reader will but compare with the places from whence you took them, he must needs be amazed, that things set down with so much eloquence and judgment, should be called in question by so great a weakness of understanding. The sentences by you alleged, "Of Speculative Doctrine" (as you call them*) are only eight, which if you had set down at large, with that coherence that he did, doubtless you could not have devised to have done Master Hooker a greater honour; but being pretermitted, by what reason I know not, you have hazarded the suspicion of intolerable ignorance. And, undoubtedly, this Article alone, giveth full assurance that this Letter could not possibly be the act of many, nor of any one, that had either charity, leisure, or learning in any great abundance. The first "Theorem" (so you term them in derision) not familiar to you common Christians, is this, "Ten the number of Nature's perfection:" In which place Master Hooker, speaking of paying of tithes, saith, "as Abraham gave voluntarily, as Jacob vowed to give God Tithes, so the Law of Moses did require at the hands of all men the self-same kind of tribute, the tenth of their corn, wine, oil, fruit, cattle, and whatsoever increase his heavenly providence should send: insomuch that Painims being herein followers of their steps, paid Tithes also.‡ Imagine we, that this was for no cause done, or that there was not some special inducement to judge the tenth of our worldly profits the most convenient for God's portion? Are not all things by him created in such sort, that the forms which give their distinction are number, their operations measure, and their matter weight? Three being the mystical number of God's unsearchable perfection within himself; Seven the number whereby our

---

* [In the margin.}   ‡ Plin. Hist. Natur. lib. xii. cap. 14.

perfections, through grace, are most ordered; and Ten the number of Nature's perfections (for the beauty of Nature is order; and the foundation of order is number; and of number, Ten the highest we can rise unto without iteration of numbers under it) could Nature better acknowledge the power of the God of Nature, than by assigning unto him that quantity which is the continent of all that she possesseth?" Now, let the Reader judge, what reason you had to mislike that he called "Ten, the number of Nature's perfections." But in this the injury you do to Master Hooker, is not all; for through his sides you wound one, upon whom, as Sixtus Senensis saith, all the commendations of the Christian Fathers are poured out; for he taketh this speech out of Philo Judæus,† in whom there are many excellent things to this purpose, and who was, in all kind of learning, incomparably the most excellent in his time; in honour of whom the ancient Romans placed his Works, as everlasting monuments in their public Library. The second is this; "*Angel's perpetuity;* the hand that draweth out celestial motion:" where, Mr. Hooker speaking of the revolution of time, which bringeth with it, a reiteration of Saint's memories, saith; "As the substance of God alone is infinite and hath no kind of limitation; so likewise his continuance is from everlasting to everlasting, and knoweth neither beginning nor end. Which demonstrable conclusion being presupposed, it followeth necessarily, that besides him, all things be finite: it cannot be but that there are bounds without the compass whereof their substance doth not extend; if in continuance also limited, they all have, it cannot be denied, their set and their certain terms, before which they had no being at all. This is the reason why, first, we do most admire those things which are greatest; and, secondly, those things which are ancientest; because the one, are less distant from the infinite substance; the other, from the infinite continuance, of God. Out of this we gather, that only God hath true immortality or eternity, that is to say, continuance wherein there groweth no difference by addition of hereafter unto now, whereas the noblest and perfectest things besides have continually,

---

† Philo Jud. lib. iv. Biblio.

through continuance, the time of former continuance lengthened; so that they could not heretofore be said to have continued so long as now, neither now so long as hereafter. God's own eternity is the hand which leadeth Angels in the course of their perpetuity; the hand, that draweth out celestial motion; the line of which motion, and the thread of time, are spun together." What could have been more excellently spoken, to have set down the frame, and dependence of things, even lineally derived from the first Motor? The third thing is this; "Church attire" (meaning Surplices) "with us, lively resembleth, the glory of Saints in heaven;" "for it suiteth fitly," saith Mr. Hooker, "with that lightsome affection of joy, wherein God delighteth when his Saints praise him; and so lively resembleth the glory of the Saints in heaven, together with the beauty wherein Angels have appeared unto men, that they which are to appear for men in the presence of God as Angels, if they were left to their own choice, and would choose any, could not easily devise a garment of more decency for such a service," Now, whosoever considereth that the Angels are said to come "out of the Temple, clothed in pure and bright linen,"† and, that the Angel at Christ's sepulchre sat "clothed in a long white garment;"‡ and, those Angels that appeared at Christ's ascension, "in white apparel;"§§ and, that white is the colour of brightness, and brightness an adjunct of "the glory of Saints," will neither deride nor mislike this speech, "that Church attire with us," "lively resembleth the glory of Saints in heaven." The fourth thing is this: "Daily bruises, Spiritual Promotions use to take, by often falling." Here you ask very sillily, "What be the bruises and falls that Spiritual Promotions, ordained by Christ do or can take?" Mr. Hooker weighing the manifold impediments which hinder the usual consultation of providing able preachers in every Parish, to instruct the people; allegeth "the multitude of parishes, the paucity of Schools, the manifold discouragements which are offered to men's inclinations that way, the penury of the Ecclesiastical estate, the irrecoverable loss of some many Livings of principal value clean taken away from the Church long since by being

---

† Rev. xv. 6.   ‡ Mark xvi. 5.   §§ Acts i. 10.

appropriated, the daily bruises that Spiritual Promotions use to take by often falling, the want of something in certain Statutes which concern the state of the Church, the too great facility of many Bishops, the stony hardness of too many patrons' hearts not touched with any feeling in this case;" who is there now, that considereth this discourse, but seeth easily the propriety of his speech, and, without an interpreter, the truth of it? That even some of the best of our spiritual preferments have received great "bruises" by often falling; where the fault hath been, that they have lighted so hard, some men know, though you and I do not. And I heartily wish, for the good of the Church, that you were able to prove, that he had spoken false in this; to the intent that our reverend Fathers, the Bishops, might be more beneficial to the inferior Clergy; more bountiful in hospitality; more honourable in their attendance; more able in their payments to their Prince; more forward in the memorable works of Devotion, building of hospitals, colleges, and such like; which, no doubt, some yet do, out of their poverty: and last of all, more conveniently provided for the avoiding of such base means as are a hindrance of Religion, a wrong to the Church and a dishonour to their profession. The next thing is this; "Multiplied petitions of worldly things, a kind of heavenly fraud, to take the souls of men as with certain baits." Where Mr. Hooker answering those, who dislike in our prayers the multiplied petitions, for earthly things saith; "It must be considered, that the greatest part of the world are they which be furthest off from perfection; such being better able by sense to discern the wants of this present life, than by spiritual capacity to apprehend things above sense which tend to their happiness in the world to come, are in that respect more apt to apply their minds, even with hearty affection and zeal at the least, unto those branches of public Prayer wherein their own particular is moved; and by this means, there stealeth upon them a double benefit. First, because that good affection, which things of smaller account have once set on work, is by so much the more easily raised higher: and, Secondly, in that the very custom of seeking so particular aid and relief at the hands of God, doth by a secret contradiction withdraw them from endeavouring to help themselves by those wicked shifts which they know can never have his allowance whose assistance their Prayer seeketh. These multiplied petitions of worldly things in prayer, have, therefore, besides their direct use, a service, whereby the Church underhand, through a kind of heavenly fraud, taketh therewith the souls of men as with certain baits." I know not, in this point, what could have been spoken, either more soundly, more plainly, or more agreeable to this purpose. And therefore it must needs be in you, either delicacy or ignorance to account this "a *Theorem* of speculative doctrine;" the very metaphor of "baits," being not unfitly applied, even by orators, to the best things. The next is these words: "In Baptism, God doth bestow presently remission of sins and the Holy Ghost, binding also himself to add, in process of time, what grace soever shall be further necessary for the attainment of everlasting life." Here you ask of Master Hooker, "What warrant he hath of present 'grace' in the very work wrought of Baptism." Where, by the way, you cunningly (with a truth of his) mingle an error of your own; for, who ever doubted but that Baptism doth bestow the "remission of sins," and yet not this, as we have often told you, for the very work wrought of Baptism. The next in these words: "The Sign of the Cross, as we use it, is in some sort a mean to work our preservation, from reproach," "and Christ's mark." It seems, that this speech hath made you to forget that civil respect, which had been fit to one whom worthily you ought to esteem, as reverend; for very rudely you say, "When, where, or how, did Christ tell thee, that 'the Sign of the Cross (as we use it)' is 'the mark of Christ,' and 'preserveth from reproach?'" Be not carried more violently than the cause requireth: for Master Hooker doth not affirm, but saith, "Shall I say?" And addeth, "surely, the mind which as yet hath not hardened itself in sin, is seldom provoked thereunto in any gross and grievous manner, but Nature's secret suggestion objecteth against it ignominy as a bar; which conceit being entered into that palace of man's fancy, the gates whereof have imprinted in them that holy Sign, which bringeth forthwith to mind whatsoever Christ hath wrought, and we vowed, against sin; it cometh hereby to pass that Christian men never want a most effectual, though a silent teacher, to avoid whatsoever may deservedly procure shame." Let us "not think it superfluous that Christ hath his mark applied unto that part where bashfulness appeareth; in token that they which are Christians should at no time be ashamed of his ignominy." The last words misliked by you, in this article are these; "Assuredly whosoever doth well observe how much all inferior things depend upon the orderly courses and motions of these greater Orbs, will hardly judge it meet or good, that the Angels assisting them should be driven to betake themselves unto other stations; although by nature they were not tied where now they are, but had charge also elsewhere; as long as their absence from beneath might but tolerably be supplied, and by descending, their rooms above should become vacant." Here, wholly mistaking Master Hooker, you run into a strange discourse of Angels, of their attendance upon the elect, and ask, "Where it is revealed, that they attend upon celestial 'Orbs;' and, whether it be not sin, to leave their natural charge?" And here you ask, whether he mean not "the Angels that fell?" These, and such like, are those collections which your judgment hath gathered, wholly mistaking the scope of this excellent speech. For he sheweth here, that there may be just reasons of Non-residence,—in Universities, in Bishops' houses, and last of all, for their employment in the families of Noblemen, or in Princes' courts. "For assuredly whosoever doth well observe, how much all inferior things depend upon the orderly courses and motions of those greater Orbs, will hardly judge it either meet or good, that the Angels assisting them should be driven to betake themselves unto other stations; although by nature they were not tied where now they are, but had charge also elsewhere; as long as their absence from beneath might but tolerably be supplied, and by descending, the rooms above should become vacant." Who understandeth not now, that by "Orbs," are meant those great persons, which by their motion do carry inferiors with them? And by "Angels assisting them," are meant those grave divines, which are by their wisdom, holiness, and direction, to moderate their motion? Why then, being but a parable, or an allegory, run you to examination of Orbs, of Angels, of Motion; and yet these are things so well known, in the Philosophers' schools, as that Master Hooker had no reason to fear to take a similitude from them without being called to examination of the truth of the thing itself. And this may suffice, for a moderate answer to those things which in this article are termed by you "Speculative Doctrine." Only I must add this, which Master Hooker noteth in a troublesome adversary with whom he had to deal, That in this article, as often in this Letter besides, there are two faults predominant, which would tire out any which would answer to every point, severally; first, unapt speaking of School controversies; and secondly, a very untoward reciting of Mr. Hookers words; that, as he which should promise to draw a man's countenance and did indeed express the parts, at least the most of them truly, but perversely place them, could not represent a more offensive visage than a man's own would be to himself; so have you dealt with Mr. Hooker, where your misplacing of those words which he hath uttered, hath framed a picture which, as you direct men to look at it, little differeth from the shape of an ugly monster: for answer whereunto, this labour is sufficient; wherein I have set down both his words and meaning in such sort, that where your accusation doth deprave the one, or that either you misinterpret, or without just cause mislike the other; it will appear so plainly, that to the indifferent reader I shall not need to add any further answer; for any man may see, that you have judged his words, as they do colours, which look upon them with green spectacles and think that which they see is green, when indeed that is green whereby they see. The best remedy will be to use charity, where judgment wanteth.

ARTICLE XIX.

OF CALVIN AND THE REFORMED CHURCHES.

Where the persons of particular men is the subject of our discourse, we cannot well either be too short or too charitable: for, of the best, if we speak much, something will be wrested to a hard construction, if uncharitably we shall seem to follow the practice of those which have no other skill to overthrow a general cause but by wounding of some particular men. And howsoever that cause must needs be weak, which either hath his [*its*] beginning, or his [*its*] greater strength, from one private man; yet doubtless in common reason, it is no small policy to blemish a truth, by detracting from the sincerity and religion of such as are the principal defenders of it. How much this part of the world hath cause to esteem of Luther, and Calvin, there is no man of any learning that can be ignorant; in which respect, notwithstanding, by some men, a threefold wrong is done unto our Church. First, to make them authors of that religion amongst us, which, by many hundred years, was far more ancient than they both were: Secondly, to lay the infirmities that were in them (as being men it were too great ignorance and flattery to acquit them from all imperfections in that kind) even upon the Religion itself; which had no more affinity with the faults that were in them, than they had with the framing of that Religion which proceeded first from no weaker author than God himself: the last, is that wrong, which our Church hath even from those who, undoubtedly, would seem in their zealous affection exceedingly to favour both. The ground of which wrong preceedeth only from hence, that those persons, and that government which place, time, and other necessities caused them to frame, ought, without exception, to be an absolute pattern to all the Churches that were round about them: insomuch, that that government, which was at the first so weak, that, without the staff of their approbation who were not subject unto it themselves, it had not brought others under subjection, began now to challenge an universal obedience, and enter into open conflict with the most Churches of Europe; but especially with those, which in desperate extremity had been relievers of it. Thus, because some few, who neither in quality nor place were much distant from Geneva, in opinion of Master Calvin, were content to follow their form of Government; others not weighing the riches of that mercy which had made their own Church too great and honourable to be framed to so narrow and poor a scantling, began stormingly to repine that presently all things were not squared to the pattern of those Churches which in their opinions were most reformed. So that, whatsoever any man spake or wrote, in disallowance of that, to be our model to be framed by, or truly to the laying open of those conflicts, (conquered with great policy) which Master Calvin had in the first establishing of that government, all sounded harshly in the ears of these men, and was plainly construed to be a direct disgracing of Master Calvin, which could be nothing else (as you say) but a discovery of a Popish and unsound affection. Where before I answer to this, I must first tell them, that if they should with the like importunity seek to frame us to the example of the primitive Church, in respect of Government, we should tell them that Israel are not bound to the same things in Canaan, that they were in the Desert; nor that those reverend Fathers the Bishops, who succeed in that apostolic charge, are not, for their maintenance and state, (though the authority be all one) to be framed to that poverty which was the portion of those who planted and governed the first Churches. This being then no such necessity, but that the Church may lawfully use even those benefits wherewith God hath blessed her, setting her feet in a large room, why should men without cause recall her back again to her days of mourning; or, feeding her with the bread of tears, coop her up in those narrow limits of subjection and want;—seeing God in his mercy hath provided for her now, the same government to be administered in a richer manner? Now, how far all men are bound to speak of those whom they reverence and love, and yet in some cases do think not safe to follow, this is that error that hath deceived many. For from hence the private oversights of those (who, how famous and excellent soever, were but men) have grown by the violence of some of their followers, to be stiffly maintained as undoubted truths; as though there were no difference betwixt being a man not always erring, and not erring at all: the one is a worthy happiness granted to some few; the other a special privilege not permitted to any,* merely man, no not to Master Calvin himself. This serveth to teach us, that for those things which we do and believe, we have better warrant than man's invention; and that no man, how excellent soever (except Christ), may, or ought precisely, to be followed in all that he doth. For thus while we add unto men that honour, a great part whereof peradventure they deserve, we detract from that Truth which we make no where to be found, but in those who inseparably are followers of their steps. That Master Calvin (who is made by you, the unpleasing subject of this article) was, (as Master Hooker termeth him,) "the wisest man incomparably, that ever the French Church did enjoy, since the hour it enjoyed him;" I think there is no man of any reading, that much doubteth: and surely, for learning, and unwearied pains in his calling, men of best judgment and understanding, would be ready enough, to give him that which belonged unto him, if some private men, out of their love and zeal, did not too greatly overload him with it. For doubtless, "we should be injurious to virtue itself, if we did derogate from them whom their industry hath made great. Two things there are of principal moment, which have deservedly procured him honour throughout all the world; the one, his exceeding pains in composing the Institution of Christian Religion, from which most have gleaned, that have written since; the other, his no less industrious travails in the exposition of holy Scripture;‡ in which two things, whosoever they were that after him bestowed their labour, he gained the advantage of prejudice

---

* "Aliud est virtutem habere, aliud nihil nisi virtutem habere." BERN.
‡ He preached yearly 286 Sermons, he read 186 Lectures every year.

132

against them if they gainsaid; and of glory above them if they consented." Now out of this (so hardly are we taught to keep a mean) proceeded this intolerable fault, That many were desirous, in an opinion of his worth, that all Churches, together with his learning, should swallow up, without making choice, whatsoever other imperfections remained in him. So that "of what account Peter Lombard was in the Church of Rome (whom for singular reverence they called the Master of the Sentences); of the same, and more, amongst the Preachers of Reformed Churches, Master Calvin was: and they only were judged the perfectest divines, which were skilfulest in Calvin's Writings. His Books almost were reputed the very Canon for controversies to be judged by." To this extremity, and far greater, the partial affection of love carried a number of wise men, who, from approbation, growing to strong praises; from praises, to admiration; from admiration, to a tyrannous opinion, that it was wholly unlawful, in any thing to dissent from him. So that now, it was almost as necessary to dispraise him, as to commend him; because, what with discretion, the Church before might have used with much profit, she scarce now could admit, without a general suspicion, through all Christendom, that we durst not in any thing dissent from him. And doubtless, in some weak minds, that which at first was but praise, in the end was not many steps short of idolatry. So that the practice of Ezekias, in breaking to pieces that serpent of brass, whereunto the children of Israel had burnt incense,‡ was not altogether unfit to be used in this case. For, in kingdoms, it is high time, either to cut off, or disgrace those, whom the multitude are willing to puff up; when (neglecting their own ruin) they are content to bury the happiness of their country, in the ashes of another's greatness. Thus, God both in mercy and judgment (in mercy to them that die, and in judgment to those that are left behind) doth, before the fulness of years, cut off those men, whom other men's erring affections have advanced too high, conveying that from the presence of unstable minds whereunto desert and weakness whilst it was in our sight, gave strength that it could bewitch. This oftentimes I

‡ 2 Kings xviii. 4.

confess hath been my private contemplation, when I have seen Parents untimely to lose their children, in whom they took most pride; Churches, whose persons of greatest ornament; the Commonwealth, those that were worthiest of all honour; as if God had been jealous that these would have stolen our honour and love from him. And therefore, wise was the answer of that mother, who in one day losing both her husband and her two sons, said, "I know, O Lord, what thou seekest, My whole love:" which she thought peradventure might have been less, if those things had been left unto her which she found herself apt for to love too much. And therefore as virtuous men have voluntarily disclosed their own infirmities (scratching as it were the face of beauty) lest others should too much admire them; so I persuade myself, that Master Calvin, if he now lived, would much worse esteem of your fond commendation, than of those speeches, which Mr. Hooker, out of judgment, doth write of him. He was doubtless, as Bishop Jewel calleth him, "a reverend Father, and a worthy ornament of God's Church;"* and surely, they do much amiss, who have sought by unjust slanders against him† (a thing too usual) to derogate from that truth, whose strength was not builded upon man's weakness. This therefore, being the practice of our adversaries, you ask Mr. Hooker, "What moved him to make choice of that worthy pillar of the Church above all other, to traduce him and to make him a spectacle before all Christians?"‡ Give me leave to answer you for him, who undoubtedly would have given a far better answer for himself, if he had lived; There is not one word that soundeth in that whole discourse, to any other end, towards Master Calvin, but to shew, how his great wisdom wrought upon their weakness; his knowledge, upon their ignorance; his gravity, upon their inconstancy; his zeal, upon their disorders; only, to establish that government, which howsoever not necessary for other places, was fit enough peradventure for that town. Neither need the present inhabitants thereof, take it in evil part, that the faultiness of their people heretofore, was by Master Hooker so far forth laid open, seeing he saith no more than their own

---

† Defence of the Apol. Part II. p. 149.   ‡ Bolsecus.

learned guides and pastors have thought necessary to discover unto the world. But "what," say you, "hath Master Calvin done against our Church, that he should be singled out as an adversary?" Surely that harm (though against his will) which never will be soundly cured, so long as our Church hath any in it to spurn at the reverend Authority of Bishops. For howsoever those Ecclesiastical Laws, established in Geneva* (wherein notwithstanding are some strange things) might be fit enough to pass for statutes, for the government of a private College, or peradventure, some small University; yet to make them a Rule, for so great, so rich, so learned a kingdom as this is, must needs be a vain desire of novelty, idly to attempt; and, a thing in nature, impossible to perform. And therefore, he cannot be free, as an occasion, though no cause, of all those troubles which have disquieted our Church for these many years. But it may be Mr. Hooker spake not thus against Mr. Calvin of himself, but persuaded either by "our adversaries, in whose mouth he is an invincible champion," or incited unto it by some of "the Reverend Fathers" of our Church; and therefore you desire him to resolve you in that point. Can it possibly be, that you should think him a man of so great simplicity, either to be moved to attempt it, by the persuasion of others, or having attempted it, that he must needs disclose it? Are all those flatterings of the Bishops; that alleging of their authorities, ended in this, To accuse them as Authors of doing that, which your conscience maketh you accuse to be evil done? Could you persuade yourself, that those Reverend Fathers, whose authorities you allege in the praise of Calvin, would be drawn to substitute another to dispraise him whom themselves commended? Is it not a thing differing from sense? void of reason? contrary to religion? And if that be a fault that Mr. Hooker is commended by our adversaries, in no construction, it can be concluded to be his fault. This peradventure, may commend them who are ready to approve learning, judgment, and moderation, even in those who are adversaries, but no way can touch those whom they thus commend: unless we make the conclusion to light heavily

---

November 12, 1557. November 13, 1561. February 19, 1560.

upon the best, both for place, wisdom, and learning, that our Church hath. Have not, in all ages, the Heathen thus commended the Christians? And did not Libanius thus think Gregory most worthy to succeed him, if he had not been a Christian? Can we in reason deny Julian his learning, because an Apostata? or Bellarmine, and others, because they have written against us? No, we willingly give them that due that belongs unto them, and hold it not unmeet to receive even from their mouths, without suspicion of treachery, that commendations which are but the recompense of a just desert. The terms of hostility are too violent and unreasonable, which deny us thus far to communicate with our very enemies. But, you say, this was pride in Mr. Hooker, to contemn all those of our own Church, as too weak to encounter with him; and therefore he must raise "Master Calvin out of his sweet bed of rest," to contend against him. And here you uncharitably make a comparison betwixt Golias and Master Hooker; only you say "unlike" in this, that Golias was content to challenge "one living" and present in the army, "demanded, but chose not; sought for one, that was alive, and vaunted not over the dead;" in all which respects by your censure, Master Hooker is more presumptuous. To speak the least which is fit to be answered in this place, surely, he which will take upon him to defend that there is no oversight in this accusation, must beware lest by such defences, he leave not an opinion dwelling in the minds of men, that he is more stiff to maintain what he hath spoken, than careful to speak nothing, but that which justly may be maintained. That he hath not shunned to encounter those, even the best of that faction in our land, yourselves can witness: that he named Mr. Calvin, only to this end, To shew the author of that Discipline which he was to handle, you must needs confess; that he rather reproved another State, than discovered the violent and uncharitable proceedings to establish it at home, it was his wisdom: for we know that the age present is corrected, when the age past is justly rebuked for the same fault.** And there cannot be a better means to cure our disorder at home, than by discovering the effects that it hath

---

** "Ætas præsens corrigitur dum præterita suis meritis objurgatur." GREGOR.

136

wrought abroad. Now, that which principally discovereth that you are not such as in the Title of this Letter, you term yourselves, is, that you make not Calvin, but Christ himself, the Author of this Discipline; who, as you say, "raised up divers men in divers places," "as Œcolampadius, Zuinglius, Suychius, Philip, Bucer, Capito, and Myconius;" "and taught them, by the same Spirit, out of the same Holy Scripture, the same doctrine and commandment of truth and righteousness." In this you bewray what you are, and how truly you favour our present State, in giving so honourable testimony of that Church government, which hath been so much oppugned by the Fathers of our Church: nay, so much misliked by the Queen herself, as appeareth by her most eloquent speech against those Reformers.‡ And, I must needs tell you, that those who have taken upon them the defence thereof, are only able to confirm it, not by places of Scripture, but by poor and marvellous slight conjectures collected from them. "I need not give instance in any one sentence so alleged, for that I think the instance of any alleged otherwise not easily to be given. A very strange thing sure it were, that such a Discipline as you speak of should be taught by Christ and his Apostles in the Word of God, and no Church ever hath found it out, nor received it till this present time; contrariwise, the government against which you bend yourselves, to be observed every where through all generations and ages of the Christian world, no Church ever perceiving the Word of God, to be against it. Find but one Church (one is not much) upon the face of the whole earth, that hath been ordered, by your discipline, or hath not been ordered by ours, that is to say, by Episcopal regiment, sithence the time that the blessed Apostles were here conversant. But you complain of it as an 'injury,'§ That men should be willed to seek for examples and patterns of governments in any of those times, that have been before." It is to small purpose, that some daughter Churches have learned to speak their mother's dialect. In one word to conclude this article, "such is naturally our affection, that whom in great things we mightily admire, in them we are not persuaded

§T.C. lib. i. p. 97.
‡ The Queen's Oration; in the Parliament, 29 Martii, 1585.

willingly that any thing should be amiss. The reason whereof is, 'that as dead flies putrify the ointment of the apothecary, so a little folly, him that is in estimation for wisdom,'* This, in every profession, hath too much authorized the judgments of a few: this with Germans hath caused Luther, and with many other Churches Calvin, to prevail in all things. But thou, O Lord, art only holy, Thou only art just, who permittest the worthiest vessels of thy glory, to be in some things blemished, with the stain of human frailty, even for this cause, lest we should esteem of any man above that which behoveth."

---

* Eccles. x. 1.

ARTICLE XX.

OF SCHOOLMEN, PHILOSOPHY, AND POPERY.

Philosophy telleth us (if it be lawful for me to use so much philosophy) that natural motions in the end are swifter, but violent are more slow; and therefore, heavy things, the lower they descend, do move faster; and, by so much also they move slower, by how much they ascend higher. It seemeth that the accusations in this Letter were such, as had their first motion, rather from the violence of some affection, than from any natural inclination to understand the Truth. For surely, though I take not upon me to censure any man (being myself clothed with so many wants), yet in my weak opinion, those, that would desire a "resolution" of such things, as "overthrow the foundation of the Church amongst us," which in your Letter you profess, should hardly esteem the right use of Philosophers and School learning, to be an accusation of that kind. So that whereas, at the first your objections seemed to move with a greater strength, now in the end, they grow weak like the stroke of a man that is half tired. But I have small reason to complain of this, which is mine own advantage: for without the armour of other learning, only in the strength of reason, I durst encounter a stronger man than myself, in this, wherein you accuse Master Hooker; that the right use of Schoolmen, and Philosophers, is no hindrance, or disgrace to true Divinity. And therefore, whereas you charge him, that "in all his discourse for, the most part, Aristotle and the ingenious Schoolmen, almost in all points have some finger;" and, "that reason is highly set up against Holy Scripture," and such like: I verily persuade myself, that herein he hath committed no unlawful thing. For those School employments are acknowledged by grave and wise men, not unprofitable to have been invented; the most approved for learning and judgment do use them without blame; the use of them hath been well liked by those that have written in this kind. The quality of the readers of his books, though not of the most, yet of those whom the matter concerned most, was such as he could not but think them of capacity very sufficient to conceive harder learning than he hath used any. The cause he had in hand, did in my opinion necessarily require those Schoolmen and philosophers that he hath used: for, where a cause is strangely mistaken, for want of distinctions, what other way was there for him, but by distinctions to lay it open, that so it might appear unto all men, whether it were consonant to truth or no? And although you and I, peradventure, being used to a more familiar and easy learning, think it unmeet to admit, approve, or frequent the Schools; yet our opinions are no Canons for Master Hooker. And, although you, being troubled in mind, do think that his writings seem like fetters, and manacles; yet no doubt he hath met both with readers and hearers more calmly affected, which have judged otherwise. But it is a strange presumption in my opinion, for private men, such as profess themselves to be but "common Christians," (which your writings, besides your own confession, do make manifest) to prescribe a form, either of writing or teaching, so plain and familiar, or rather indeed so empty and shallow, that no man may doubt, how unlearned soever, to give his censure. Must all knowledge be humbled so low that it must stoop to the capacity of the meanest reader? But the Fathers,† say you, have misliked it. Indeed I confess, there is an overmuch use, which is evil in all things where there is not an absolute necessity. Besides, things comparatively spoken, in regard of true understanding of the Scriptures, is no rule for warrant that they are to be misliked simply. For Stapleton himself confesseth, in his caustions of expounding the Scripture, that the Schoolmen have not a certain, and infallible authority of interpreting; which as to maintain must needs be great simplicity, so to

---

† Cranmer, Luther.   § Lib. x. cap. 11.   ¶ [The old form of the verb plural.]

dislike all use of them is intolerable unthankfulness.§ But, in this accusation, it is not apparent what you mean, when you allege out of Luther, "that School-divinity hath banished from us the true and sincere divinity." If this were the direct judgment of Luther, to condemn all School-divinity; yet it is a strange opposition to allege the sentence of one man against the practice and authorities of the best Fathers. Neither do we understand which it is (the old or new) that so much offends you; by old, we mean that scholastical kind of expounding, which the most eloquent Fathers lately comen‡ from the Schools of Rhetoricians, and Philosophers, have brought with them, to the interpreting of Holy Scriptures; that thus they might be able to teach, to delight, to persuade; a matter fitting all, but not easy for any that is not excellently furnished with human learning. In this sense Beda calleth Prudentius the most noble Schoolman of the Spaniards,* whom it is like, in the severity of your judgment, you would have dispraised; and Gennadius, in the Catalogue of famous writers, reckoneth up Musæus, Julianus, Eucherius, and divers others, amongst the Schoolmen; that is, amongst the chief professors of School eloquence. Saint Jerome affirmeth of himself, that many things in Divinity, he handled with School ornament; and of St. Paul he saith, that when he preached at Athens, upon occasion of the inscription of the Altar to the unknown God, he handled it with a scholastical kind of elegancy.† Is this, then, that which so much offends you? Was it an ornament in these Fathers, and many others, and is it a blemish in Mr. Hooker? But peradventure it is the new and later kind of School interpreting that you mislike; whose method is Philosophical disputing, made of Aristotelian learning; this sprang up about some four hundred and odd years past,‡ in the time of Lotharius the second, Emperor of Rome; who, recovering out of darkness the Roman Laws, caused them publicly to be read, and to be expounded by divers Writers; by this means Divinity began to wax cold, until by imitation of these men, certain devout Monks, and others, undertook the like in

---

* In lib. De Arte metr. nobilissimum Hispanorum Scholasticum.
†In Com. Epist. ad Titum.   ‡ An. 1130.

expounding the holy Scripture; by which means even until this day, there remaineth in the Schools ten orders of their usual expounding; by Concordance, History, Postil, Question, Lecture, Compendium or Abridgment, Sermon, Metre, Meditation;§ all which, no doubt of it, in your opinion are esteemed unlawful and unprofitable: now, many that were excellent in this kind, the Church both knoweth how to use with great profit, and in recompense of their labour, hath given them titles, with much honour. Thus, Alexander Hales, who made his Summe, that excellent work, by commandment of Innocentius the fourth, was called "the fountain of life,"‖ because of that lively knowledge that flowed from him: he was Master to Bonaventure, a scholar not inferior to himself, of whom he was wont to say, That in Bonaventure he thought Adam sinned not; meaning for that illumination, which was in him (and doubtless there was much in him) as though he had not been darkened by the fall of Adam; and therefore the Church called him "the Seraphical Doctor." To these Aquinas was not inferior, who came so near unto St. Austin, that some thought he had all his Works by heart, and by a common proverb it was spoken, that the soul of St. Austin dwelt in Aquinas; in whom above all the rest, four contrarieties were said to excel; abundance, brevity, facility, security: in respect whereof, he gained the title to be called "Angelical."* Now for any man to follow the steps of these, though treading sure, as having more light, can any man in reason account it to be a fault? Is there no other matter of reproof in Master Hooker's Writings, but that virtues must be faults? But he seeketh to prove matters of divinity with the strength of "reason:" Indeed this is a great fault, which if many had not been afraid to commit, the world had not been filled with so many idle and unreasonable discourses. But so it is, that through an ignorant zeal of honoring the Scriptures, the name of "the light of nature," is made hateful with men; the star of reason, and learning, and all other such like helps, beginneth no otherwise to be thought of, than as if it were an unlucky comet; or, as if God had so accursed it, that it should never shine, or give light in things

---

§ Sixt. Sin. Bib. Sanct. lib. iii. p. 180.   ‖ Fons vitæ.   * Moritur, ætat. 48. A.D. 1274.

concerning our duty any way toward him; but be esteemed as that "star," in the Revelation called "wormwood:"‡ which, being fallen from heaven, maketh rivers and waters, in which it falleth so "bitter" that men tasting them, die thereof. A number there are, who think they cannot admire, as they ought, the power and authority of the Word of God, if, in things divine, they should attribute any force to man's Reason; for which cause they never use reason so willingly, as to disgrace reason. Their usual and common discourses are to this effect; *Object.* 1. "The natural man perceiveth not the things of the Spirit of God; for they are foolishness unto him; neither can he know them, because they are spiritually discerned."§—For answer whereunto, we say, That concerning the ability of Reason, to search out and to judge of things Divine, if they be such as those properties of God, and those duties of men towards him which may be conceived by attentive consideration of heaven and earth, we know that of mere natural men, the Apostle testifieth, how they know both God and the law of God;‖ other things of God there be which are neither so found, nor though they be shewed, can ever be approved without the special approbation of God's good grace and Spirit: such is the suffering and rising again of our Saviour Christ, which Festus, a mere natural man, could not understand;¶ therefore Paul seemed in his eyes to be learnedly "mad."** This sheweth, that nature hath need of grace,†† to which Master Hooker was never opposite, in saying that grace may have use of nature. *Object.* 2. But Paul chargeth the Colossians to "beware of Philosopy,‡‡ that is to say, such knowledge as men, by natural Reason are able to attain.—I confess, "Philosophy" we are warned to take heed of; not that Philosophy, which is true and sound knowledge, attained by a natural discourse of reason; but that Philosophy, which to bolster heresy, or error, (which I am sure Master Hooker doth not) casteth a fraudulent shew of reason upon things which are indeed unreasonable; and, by that means, as by a stratagem, spoileth the simple

---

‡ Rev. viii. 10, 11.   §1 Cor. ii. 14.   ‖ Rom. ii. 14.
¶ Acts xxv. 19, 20.   **Acts xxvi. 24.   ††1 Cor. ii. 24.   ‡‡ Col. ii. 8.

which are not able to withstand such cunning. He that giveth warning to take heed of an enemy's policy, doth not give counsel to avoid all policy; but rather, to use all provident foresight and circumspection, lest our simplicity be overreached by cunning sleights. The way not to be inveigled by them that are so guileful through skill, is thoroughly to be instructed in that which maketh skilful against guile; and to be armed with that true and sincere Philosophy, which doth teach against that *deceitful* and *vain* which *spoileth*. *Object.* 3. But have not the greatest troublers of the Church been the greatest admirers of human reason? Hath their deep and profound skill in secular learning made them the more obedient to the truth, and not armed them rather against it?—Indeed, many great philosophers have been very unsound in belief, and yet many, sound in belief, have been great philosophers. Could secular knowledge bring the one sort unto the love of Christian Faith? nor [*or*] Christian Faith, the other sort out of love with secular knowledge? The harm that Heretics did, was to such as by their weakness were not able to discern between sound and deceitful reasoning; and the remedy against it was ever, the skill of the ancient Fathers to discover it. Insomuch that Cresconius the heretic complained greatly of St. Austin, as you do of Master Hooker, for being too full of logical subtitles. *Object.* 4. But the Word of God in itself is absolute, exact, and perfect, and therefore needless to add any human or School learning; for those weapons are like the armour of Saul, rather cumbersome than needful; and with these hath Master Hooker filled his writings.—I answer, there is in the world no kind of knowledge whereby any part of truth is seen, but we justly account it precious: yea, that principal Truth, in comparison whereof all other truth is vile, may receive from it some kind of light; whether it be that Egyptian, and Chaldean "wisdom" mathematical, wherewith Moses* and Daniel† were furnished; or that natural, moral, and civil wisdom, wherein Solomon excelled all men;‡ or that rational and oratorical

---

* Acts vii. 22. † Dan. i. 17. ‡ 1 Kings iv. 29, 30.
§ Acts xxii. 3. ‖ [1 Tim. vi. 16.]

wisdom of the Grecians, which the Apostle St. Paul brought from Tarsus; or that Judaical which he learned in Jerusalem, sitting at the feet of Gamaliel:§ to detract from the dignity thereof, were to injure even God himself; who, being that "light which none can approach unto,"‖ hath sent out these lights, whereof we are capable, as so many sparkles resembling the bright fountain from which they rise. And therefore, unto the Word of God, being in respect of that end whereunto God ordained it, perfect, exact, and absolute, we do not add any thing as a supplement of any maim, or defect therein; but as a necessary instrument, without which we could not reap by the Scripture's perfection, that fruit, and benefit which it yieldeth. In respect of all which places alleged, it must needs seem strange, that any for the use of School divinity, and human learning, should incur that hard suspicion, which you seek to fasten upon Mr. Hooker; namely, that he is "a privy and subtle enemy to the whole state of our Church; that he would have men to deem her Majesty to have done ill in abolishing the Romish Religion; that he would be glad to see the back-sliding of all Reformed Churches;" or, that he means "to bring in a confusion of all things;" a toleration "of all religions; these, and such like, are the heavy conclusions that follow the use of Schoolmen and secular Learning; and the least of those evils, which are likely, in your opinion, to be derived into the heart of our Church and Commonwealth, from that dangerous poison which is contained in Master Hooker's Writings. Surely it is great pity, that all men should "think what they list, or speak openly what they think;" but doubtless it did little move him, when you say that which a greater than you certainly will gainsay. His words in this cause have seemed to you as an arrow sticking in a thigh of flesh, and your own as a child whereof you must needs be delivered by an hour; but deliberation would have given, peradventure, more ripeness, which now by haste hath, as a thing born out of time, been small joy to you that begat it. Therefore I will conclude with the speech of the son of Sirach: "He that applieth his mind to the law of the most High, keepeth the sayings of famous men, and entereth in, also, into the secrets of dark sentences: he seeketh out the mystery of grave sentences, and exerciseth himself in dark parables; though he be dead he shall leave a greater fame, than a thousand."§ Doubtless this is verified in him of whom you have published unto the world so hard a censure.

---

§ Eccles. xxxix. 1-3, 11.

ARTICLE XXI.

THE STYLE AND MANNER OF WRITING.

As it is an honour to perform that which is excellent; so, it is a virtue to approve that which is excellently performed: where to be wanting in the first, may be sloth, or ignorance, but to be wanting in the latter, must needs be malice. Few there are or have been in any age, which reaping the due recompense of their labour, have done that good which they ought, and have not received that reward which they ought not. Wise men have thought no otherwise, but that this common lot might be their portion; yet the fear thereof could not have that power over all, to make them in that respect wholly and unprofitably silent: knowing, that even that which they suffered for well doing, was their honour; and that which they did well and suffered for it, was others' shame. This vice, in my opinion, is not more usual with any, than with us, who by reason of the corrupt quality thereof, have imposed a silence to a great number, who by their writings, doubtless, would have been very singular ornaments unto God's Church. Whereas strangers of less merit, have a twofold advantage. The one, that we read their writings without prejudice of their persons; the other, that with a desire of novelty, we greedily devour (as we do fashions) whatsoever we think to be done by strangers; this only, in all things (how excellent soever) being cause enough of dislike, that it is homeborn; but more justly of silence, that it is disliked. So that when we have sifted, whatsoever is likely to be reproved, even the last thing to be examined is the Style itself. Thus have you dealt with Master Hooker, whom, as in all other things, you have set upon the rack; so in this,

148

you have taken upon you far more than beseemeth either the modesty or the small learning that is usually found in such as profess themselves to be but "common Christians." For certainly to judge of a Style, is not the least point of learning, though it be the least known: but, peremptorily, to dislike, which you do, is more than only to judge. For this is but to deliver special verdict, as we think ourselves; but the other is to take upon us, exactly to tell what the law is. Some I have seen, excellently writing upon the variety of styles; and the best, in my opinion, is one Pascal, who was like enough to judge well, because he himself wrote an excellent style; yet surely there is in no point of learning greater variety of tastes than there is in this: some prefer Sallust, others Cæsar, a third Seneca, a fourth Tacitus; in one word, every man according to his own fancy. This, as it is in Styles, so it is in the several actions of men; where they are no sooner born into the world, but Censure, as a gossip, names them. A thing I confess needful, and unfit to be prohibited, seeing we reap oftentimes, more benefit by our enemies than our friends; yet this sheweth that the world is unhappy, where the best offices are performed by our worst acquaintance. If we come to Authors, some dislike Plato, as Athenæus did, calling him "confused;" others say, I only esteem Plato, who doth so cunningly weave knowledge and virtue together, as if he said, he were content to give you knowledge, upon condition, that you should be honest. Some compared Aristotle to that fish, whose humour is like ink;** Livy he likes not Trogus, nor Tully, Demosthenes; Lenæus a servant of Pompey's mislikes Sallust; Asinius calleth him "an affecter;" Quintilian calleth Seneca "chalk without sand;" Caligula dispraised Livy as "full of words," and yet negligent, in suppressing the triumphs of Romulus, gotten by the victory of the Tuscans. Thus Varro (without question a man most learned, even in the opinion of St. Austin,) by one Quintus Rhemius Palemon was called a "hog." Surely emulation of learning, and difference either of opinion or manners, breeds a dislike in scholars. This hath been, is, and shall be that evil, whereunto learned men

---

** Sepia, a Cuttle.

must be subject in the variety of other men's censures; nay even those books, which we translate because they are excellent, others wish, because they are excellent not to be translated. Surely it is much easier, saith Dio. Cassius, to reprehend others, than to moderate ourselves.† Some are of so feeble and weak stomachs, that they loathe bread: nay some are of that inconstant humour, that what they commend now, they dispraise the next day; and what yesterday they dispraised, they commend to-day. For in the beginning of your Letter, you call it a "sweet sound" of Mr. Hooker's "melodious style;" and in another place, you confess that his books are "very excellently and learnedly penned" and yet in this Article, your last scruple is, because his Books are so long and tedious, in a Style not usual, and as you think, the like hard to be found. Where, it seems, you are desirous to reprehend, if you could but resolve of the manner how. I dare not take upon me to censure those, whom you say he is unlike; "Cranmer, Ridley, Latimer, Jewel, Whitgift, Fox, Fulke:" but I persuade myself, that whatsoever their other virtues were, wherein peradventure they were more eminent, yet doubtless the best of them that now liveth, will acknowledge Mr. Hooker's style to be very excellent. And although it is unmeet I should compare him with others whose labours have been profitable in another kind, yet I hope I may say without offence, that as profoundly to judge, with sound variety of all learning, was common to him with divers others; so, to express what he conceived, in the eloquence of a most pure style, was the felicity almost of himself alone. That honourable Knight, Sir Philip Sidney, gave a taste in an argument of recreation,* how well that style would befit an argument of a graver subject; which it may be is more unpleasing in the taste of some, because the manner is learned, and the subject is not agreeing to their humour. Doubtless, the perfecting of a style, and especially of our English style (which in my opinion, refuseth not the purest ornaments of any language) hath many mo [*more*] helps than those honourable places of learning, the Universities, can afford. And therefore, in those things, which they conceive (and

† Hist. lib. xxxvi.   * [His "Arcadia." See Vol. I. p. xii. Note.]

some of them conceive much) there are found, in the Prince's Court, divers most purely eloquent, whom even the best in the Universities may despair to imitate. And (if I may speak without offence), I am fully persuaded, that Mr. Hooker's style (if he had had less learning; a strange fault, for the weight of his learning made it too heavy;) had been incomparably the best that ever was written in our Church. If our English Story had been born to that happiness, ever to have been attired in such rich ornaments, she might worthily have been entertained in the best Courts that the world hath; but, all Countries know, our actions have been better done, than they have been told. Of things affected we may give a reason, but to ask, as you do, a reason of Mr. Hooker, for his style, it is all one, as if you asked him why he knew so much. For doubtless out of judgment he made this choice (in my weak opinion, or strong fancy) simply the best, and (without comparison) imitable to few. Therefore, your comparison of the bramble was unfit, which by a shew deceived you "afar off;" for there is much more by a narrow view to be discerned in him, than he seemeth to promise at the first sight. "Three things" you desire "with all instancy: First, to shew what arguments he hath alleged, which are not to be found in the Answer of that Reverend Father unto Mr. Cartwright." To satisfy you in this demand, if there were no difference, yet the consent of their arguments were reason enough, for you to allow Mr. Hooker, seeing you have given your approbation of the works of that most Reverend Father, whose worthiness no doubt, can receive little honour from your praise; yet you know, that the whole subject of Mr. Hooker's first four Books, is an argument, as, full of learning, so, directly heretofore not handled by any, that I know. Secondly, you desire, that if he "set forth his other books, which are promised, that he would be more plain, and sensible." Concerning those three Books of his, which from his own mouth, I am informed that they were finished, I know not in whose hands they are; nor, whether the Church shall ever be bettered by so excellent a Work; for as the Church might have been happy, if he had lived to have written more, so she were not altogether so much harmed, if she might but enjoy what he hath written. But for you to prescribe him a style, as it is an authority unfit to assume unto yourself, so it were a request, if he lived, impossible to obtain. For as once the greatest of place for judgment of Law in our Land§ answered a client of his in my hearing, who was desirous to have him take information of his cause, from another lawyer that seemed more fully acquainted with it; "he will speak," saith he, "well himself, by his own direction; but if I should speak by his information I should speak but like a fool:" so I am sure, howsoever you yourself may write, following your own style, yet Master Hooker by your direction could hardly attain the commendations that himself had already gained. Lastly, you wish him to "be careful not to corrupt the English Creed, by philosophy or vain deceit, of Schoolmen's new-born divinity:" give me leave to exempt you from this fear; for I am fully persuaded, never any man lived, who would have been lother to have been the author of any new and unwarranted opinion which might give but the least shew of contradiction to the Faith which our Church professeth. Things are not to be measured by violence of speech, or uncharitable collections; for who are on God's side, and who against, our Lord, in his good time, shall reveal. And, seeing you doubt of his soundness so far (that because he maketh the Church of Rome a part of the Church of Christ (which Mr. Saravia, Zanchy, and others do, that you wish him to take heed, that he forget not to give his "lawful Sovereign her right and full due") give me leave to set down his words, and in his words his sound and fervent affection in this point. "When the ruins of the House of God, (that House which consisting of religious souls, is most immediately the precious Temple of the Holy Ghost) were become not in his sight alone, but in the eyes of the whole world so exceeding great, that very Superstition began even to feel itself too far grown; the first that with us made way to repair the decays thereof, was King Henry the Eighth; the son and successor of which famous King, as we know , was Edward the Saint. In whom (for so by the event we may gather) it pleased God, righteous and just, to let England see what a blessing sin and iniquity would not suffer her to enjoy; that work, which the one had begun and the

---

§ The Lord Keeper.

other so far proceeded in, was in short space so overthrown, as if almost it had never been; till such time as the God, whose property is to shew his mercies then greatest when they are nearest to be utterly despaired of, caused in the depth of discomfort and darkness a most glorious Star to arise, and on her head settled the Crown, whom he himself had kept as a lamb from the slaughter of those bloody times; that the experience of his goodness in her own deliverance might cause her merciful disposition to take so much the more delight in saving others whom the like necessity should press;‡ the continuance of which mercy towards us, in the abundance of his favour to her, we wish may happily continue so long as the sun endureth. Hitherto Master Hooker. To conclude this small and imperfect work, whereas you join these Books of Master Hooker, with two other which you take to be "bellows to blow the coals of sedition;" I persuade myself, that the ages which are to come, shall more than the present, esteem them with high honour. For mine own part, what I have done in defence thereof, it is neither from opinion of sufficiency, who know mine own strength in this kind, weaker than many thousands; nor, from a desire of contention, which I hold (howsoever sometimes needful) the worst employment of all learning; nor from a willingness to flatter any, a fault (whatsoever my other infirmities are) whereunto I was never subject; nor that I thought those would have been wanting, who had both far more learning and greater reason, to undertake the Defence than myself had. Wherefore, if there be any thing, either unsoundly, or uncharitably set down (faults, which willingly I would be loath to be accused of) I submit myself to the Judgment of the Church, and the courteous admonition of the Christian Reader. But, if any man without cause, spurn or think himself grieved, and find that contained herein which with judgment and sound learning he is able to confute, and be desirous hereafter to receive my answer, let him set to his name that writeth; otherwise, let him think, that Libels, personal, and of no moment, are to be rather punished by Authority, than confuted by any man's pen. And so I will heartily

---

‡ *Querimonia Ecclesiæ.* Book of Scotizing and Genevatizing.

pray that no strife may ever be heard of again, but this, Who shall hate strife most, who shall pursue peace and unity with most desire.

INDEX

TEXTS AND STUDIES IN RELIGION

40. Susan Drain, **The Anglican Church in Nineteenth Century Britain: Hymns Ancient and Modern (1860-1875)**

41. Aegidius of Rome, **On Ecclesiastical Power: De Ecclesiastica Potestate**, Arthur P. Monahan (trans.)

42. John R. Eastman, **Papal Abdication in Later Medieval Thought**

43. Paul Badham,(ed.), **Religion, State, and Society in Modern Britain**

44. Hans Denck, **Selected Writings of Hans Denck, 1500-1527**, E.J. Furcha (trans.)

45. Dietmar Lage, **Martin Luther's Christology and Ethics**

46. Jean Calvin, **Sermons on Jeremiah by Jean Calvin**, Blair Reynolds (trans.)

47. Jean Calvin, **Sermons on Micah by Jean Calvin**, Blair Reynolds (trans.)

48. Alexander Sándor Unghváry, **The Hungarian Protestant Reformation in the Sixteenth Century Under the Ottoman Impact: Essays and Profiles**

49. Daniel B. Clendenin and W. David Buschart (eds.), **Scholarship, Sacraments and Service: Historical Studies in Protestant Tradition, *Essays in Honor of Bard Thompson***

50. Randle Manwaring, **A Study of Hymn-Writing and Hymn-Singing in the Christian Church**

51. John R. Schneider, **Philip Melanchthon's Rhetorical Construal of Biblical Authority: Oratio Sacra**

52. John R. Eastman (ed.), **Aegidius Romanus, *De Renunciatione Pape***

53. J.A. Loubser, **A Critical Review of Racial Theology in South Africa: The Apartheid Bible**

54. Henri Heyer, **Guillaume Farel: An Introduction to His Theology**, Blair Reynolds (trans.)

55. James E. Biechler and H. Lawrence Bond (ed.), **Nicholas of Cusa on Interreligious Harmony: Text, Concordance and Translation of *De Pace Fidei***

56. Michael Azkoul, **The Influence of Augustine of Hippo on the Orthodox Church**

57. James C. Dolan, **The *Tractatus Super Psalmum Vicesimum* of Richard Rolle of Hampole**

58. William P. Frost, **Following Joseph Campbell's Lead in the Search for Jesus' Father**

59. Frederick Hale, **Norwegian Religious Pluralism: A Trans-Atlantic Comparison**

60. Frank H. Wallis, **Popular Anti-Catholicism in Mid-Victorian Britain**